You Can't Fly If You're Still Clutching the Dirt

How to Stop Worrying & Achieve Your God-Given Potential

by Marnie L. Pehrson

Cover Design by Tamara Ingram

Published by CES Business Consultants
514 Old Hickory Ln * Ringgold GA 30736
Tel: 706-866-2295
www.MarniePehrson.com
www.SheLovesGod.com

ISBN: 0-9729750-8-X

For my children: Laurel, Caleb, Joshua, Jillian, Nathaniel, and Elijah. May you find the exhilarating joy and peace that comes to those who obediently trust the Lord, release their worries, and fly!

Table of Contents

Introduction

Life is too short to waste it worrying. As the old saying goes, "A person who worries about death, dies a thousand times while the rest of us must only die once." I come from a long line of worriers, and it's been one of my quests in life to find a cure. Wouldn't it be wonderful never to worry again? Wouldn't it be fantastic if you didn't have to live in fear? What if I told you it was possible!

There is a cure for worry, and it doesn't involve drugs. Granted, some people, through no fault of their own, are prone to worry for chemical or genetic reasons, but I'm not one of those people. While I believe this book could even be useful for someone with a mental disorder, this book is written for the average person. It's written for all those people out there like me who have a bad habit of worrying because that's what we grew up watching our mothers do.

The cure for worry begins where worry lives
– in our thoughts.

Worry comes when we do not trust in a happy
ending. It comes when we're afraid we won't have
enough of what we need at the right time and in the
right place. It plagues our minds when we don't trust
that God is looking out for our best interests. Or
perhaps we fear He's not taking care of our loved
ones. We may believe that things will work out for
our good (Romans 8:28), but we're not convinced
we're going to like where God's taking us! Sort of like
how medicine is good for you, but it still tastes bad.
We worry when we look at our existence as a single-
act play and do not realize that we are eternal beings
with eternal promise!

Bottom line, worry comes when we feel like
things are out of our control. We might know what
we want, but when is it going to happen? How is it
possible? Where will it happen? Who will be
involved? The uncertainty in these questions plagues
the fretting mind. The natural outcome for this type
of thinking usually leads to struggling and
manipulating people and circumstances until we've
made a mess.

When we worry, we waste valuable creative time
that we could be spending learning new skills,
developing talents and reaching our full God-given
potential! Worry is destructive. It fritters away time.

It kills creativity and it often is a prophet of its own self-fulfilling doom. Most of all worry keeps us from claiming the blessings God has for us. It prevents us from living up to the fullness of our creation and finding joy in life. Why? Because faith and fear cannot occupy the mind simultaneously. If faith is "the substance of things hoped for," then worry is the substance of things dreaded (Hebrews 3:6).

The premise of this book is that worry could be eliminated if

· we believed that there is no scarcity but only abundance;

· we trusted God that not only is He looking out for our best interests, but also that we will be thrilled with where He's taking us;

· we knew without a doubt that we could have any righteous desire of our hearts;

· we understood with crystal clarity what portion of life is within our control and what part is under God's;

· we knew how to stop whining and intelligently and specifically ask for solutions.

Within the pages of this book, you will learn a clear method for replacing doubt, fear and worry with hope, faith, and peace. As a result, you will be ready to find the joy that is only available to those who strive for and reach their full God-given potential, completely unfettered by the limiting chains of fear and worry.

Chapter 1:
You Were Born to Fly!

The Parable of the Cat Bird

When I was a small child, my father found a cat bird inside the house. It frantically flew about, bouncing into walls and windows until he finally caught it. He held it tightly. At first the bird struggled for freedom, squawking, scratching, clawing and crying to be released. The harder the bird struggled, the more my father held onto it, restricting its movements to keep it from injuring itself further.

My father didn't want to keep the bird tightly bound. He would rather let it move about freely. But for the safety of the bird, he needed to keep it confined within his hands. The bird struggled for some time and then finally began to sense that my father meant it no harm. When it quit struggling, he relaxed his hold on it. If it fought, his hands once again became confining. Eventually, the bird completely relaxed, and my father set it on the kitchen floor, and it toddled about. By the time the bird could be set free, they had become friends. They had come to trust one another.

My dad took the bird outside and held open his hand for it to go back to its natural habitat, but it wouldn't leave. Instead it waddled around in his hand, climbed up his arm and perched on my dad's shoulder. It didn't want to leave him! Finally my father set it on a porch railing. Reluctantly, after some time, the bird joined its friends in the trees. Even then it perched in a nearby tree and chirped merrily talking to my father for quite some time.

My father tells this story every now and then, and I've always felt it held some significance about life, about a principle of freedom and gaining trust. Most recently, I've come to see the symbolism of how our Heavenly Father deals with us. Like my father, our Heavenly Father is there to help and protect us. He too wants us free to fly and explore the full potential of our divine creation. But often we're like that injured bird, trapped inside a house. We squirm, fight, claw and squawk, but in our wounded condition, our Heavenly Father holds us tightly, restricting our movements.

Just as the bird fought to escape in the beginning, we too fight and claw to reach our goals and aspirations. Like the bird trapped in the house, inside our own limiting borders, our Heavenly Father knows it's not possible yet. It's neither the time nor the place. We must first learn to relax and fully trust Him. Only then, when He's confident that our mad scramble for control will not cause us to injure ourselves further, does He relax His grip.

Once we calm down and trust Him fully, He opens His palm and sets us free to explore a little. Interestingly enough, at this point, when we've come to love and trust the Father, our goals and aspirations don't seem so important anymore. But our Heavenly Father hasn't held us just so He can confine us. No! Now that we've learned how to trust, relax and communicate with Him, He wants us outside so we can fly! He wants us to fill the measure of our creation in a great big world that He created! Ultimate happiness and joy only come for us and Him as we learn to trust Him enough so He can completely liberate us from the confines of our own limiting beliefs and boundaries.

You Are a Joint-Heir with Christ

In John 10:10 Jesus says, "I am come that they might have life and that they might have it more abundantly."

What is abundance? A trip to the dictionary will tell you that abundance is a great plentiful amount, fullness to overflowing, or affluence and wealth. In the framework of this book, I'm building on a very important premise. That foundation is that as a child of God, your Father in Heaven has a divine plan for your life. You have a God-ordained mission to fulfill, and it is His desire to give you everything you need to do that.

In the very first chapter of Genesis, verse 26 God lays down a defining fact about who we are: "And God said, Let us make man in our image, after our likeness: and let them have dominion over the fish of the sea, and over the fowl of the air, and over the cattle, and over all the earth, and over every creeping thing that creepeth upon the earth."

Mankind (men and women) are made in the image of God, after His likeness. We are modeled after our Creator, and we have access to and dominion over the things of this earth in order that we may live according to our Creator's divine plan. We are higher than the animals. We have the ability to choose for ourselves. Paul testified to the Romans, "The Spirit itself beareth witness with our spirit, that we are the children of God: And if children, then heirs; heirs of God, and joint-heirs with Christ" (Romans 8: 16-17).

We were born to become joint-heirs with Christ. We were created for higher things than the animals. When we can get a handle on that and really understand this principle, our lives will transform. Repeatedly throughout scripture the Lord teaches us of our infinite worth. He teaches this principle through illustrations in the lives of those who followed Him.

"All scripture is given by inspiration of God, and is profitable for doctrine, for reproof, for correction, for instruction in righteousness: That the man of God may be perfect, throughly furnished unto all good works" (2 Timothy 3:16-17). The examples we find in scripture are there to teach us how to become "perfect" or "mature" and furnished unto "good works." God's power that works through us – His enabling grace – gives us the ability to accomplish great things. We are not alone. We may be imperfect, human, and flawed, but Jesus Christ is perfect. His grace and atonement is infinite. When we partner with Him, nothing that is expedient in Christ is impossible for us. Nothing is outside our grasp with Him on our side. This is an amazing power that we are able to tap into when we humble ourselves, come unto Christ, and live up to our God-given potential.

When we come unto Christ, we become perfected in Him as we deny ourselves of all ungodliness. When we love God with all our might, mind and strength, His grace transforms us. His grace is more than sufficient to perfect our imperfections, strengthen our weaknesses, repair our flaws and enable us to abound in good works. Repeatedly throughout scripture we see this happen to ordinary men and women.

Look at the heroes and heroines of the Bible. They were just normal people. What made them extraordinary is that they loved God and sought to live their lives in accordance with His will. Their stories were documented to teach us lessons about ourselves. If we liken their stories to our own we learn that just as Esther, Noah, Jeremiah, Isaiah, John the Baptist, Paul and others had specific missions to fulfill, so do we.

Without the precise positioning of Esther as Queen, the Jews would have been slaughtered. Without righteous Noah and his family, who would have repopulated the earth after the flood destroyed the wicked? Would the people have been prepared for Christ if there had been no John the Baptist to advise them that the Messiah would soon come and that they should prepare their hearts through repentance and baptism?

The Lord told Jeremiah, "Before I formed thee in the belly I knew thee; and before thou camest forth out of the womb I sanctified thee, and I ordained thee a prophet unto the nations." (Jeremiah 1:5). The Lord would say no less of you or me. Perhaps we were not ordained to be prophets, but we were ordained to other tasks – mothers, fathers, teachers, and living examples of Christ-like lives. Paul taught that "He hath chosen us in Him before the foundation of the world" (Ephesians 1:4, see also Job 38:4-7).

Each of us is known to Him, and we've been known to Him for a long time before we were even born. It is no coincidence that the Lord told the Israelites when they entered the Promised Land to "Distress not the Moabites, neither contend with them in battle" (Deuteronomy 2:9). The Lord did not wish them utterly destroyed as so many of the neighboring inhabitants of Canaan were. For He well knew that in a future generation Ruth the Moabitess would one day travel with her mother-in-law, Naomi, back to the land of the Israelites, accept the God of Israel, marry Boaz, and become the great-great-grandmother of King David through whose lineage would come the Son of God.

Just as God cleared the way for devoted Ruth, God has cleared a path for you. "The steps of a good man [or woman] are ordered by the Lord: and he delighteth in his/her way" (Psalms 37: 23).

You may or may not have discovered your God-given mission. But in order to discover it and fulfill it, you need certain things. You need God's abundance in your life. You may need an abundance of knowledge, education, time, energy, resources, connections, or even money to fulfill your mission.

In my life, I've been blessed with an abundance of children, friends, family, land, and ideas. I'm also surprised at the abundance of knowledge, answers and talents that the Lord is more than willing to share with us when we're seeking first to build the kingdom of God and promote righteousness on the earth. Your abundance could be in different areas than mine, but when you are on the Lord's path for your life you can expect an abundance of everything you need to accomplish your righteous desires. The earth is full and there is plenty to spare. There is no scarcity. There is only abundance. Christ is about abundance, and Satan pushes the false belief that scarcity rules – that only an elite few may be saved or only a privileged minority may be blessed with the abundance of the earth. He knows that this false belief makes us fearful and selfish and stalls our progression.

The gate is strait and the way is narrow such that few there be that find it because few will humble themselves and follow Christ (Matthew 7:14). It is not because God wants only a few to follow Christ or that he wants only a few to be on the path! And it certainly isn't because there isn't enough room for everyone! Christ says that He was lifted up that he might draw **all** unto Him (John 12:32). There is plenty with God. It is we who limit ourselves.

Too many people never fulfill their God-given potential to their fullest degree because they do not know the principles and laws surrounding abundance. They do not understand that the Lord fully intends and WANTS to give you everything you need to fulfill your mission. They believe that God wants you to suffer privation and lack in order that you may remain humble, when in reality nothing could be further from the truth. Examples abound in scripture that illustrate that when people followed God and lived His commandments, they prospered and received a "Promised Land." It is when they become proud, arrogant and begin to believe that it is their own ingenuity and wisdom that made them successful that they fall. Pride certainly goes before a fall (Proverbs 16:18). And ingratitude goes before pride. Men and women bring upon themselves their own destruction.

God wants to bless those who follow Him. The Lord taught Joshua that the path to happiness and success lay in meditating and following the word of God: "This book of the law shall not depart out of thy mouth; but thou shalt meditate therein day and night, that thou mayest observe to do according to all that is written therein: for then thou shalt make thy way prosperous and then thou shalt have good success" (Joshua 1:8).

Still, many believe that God wants to hold them back and keep them unsuccessful. If this were true, why would God tell Joshua how to become successful if He didn't want him to do it?

The truth is that the Lord wants you to have all the resources, talents, knowledge, experience, energy, associations, and time that you need to build His kingdom in the unique way that only you can. He wants you to be successful!

No one else can take your place. Think of the honey bee. It goes about its work, doing what it is created to do and in the process it pollinates the flowers and vegetation and produces sweet honey for mankind. Just as the honey bee is never fully aware of the great good and rippling effect of its day-to-day tasks, when we fill our mission we send forth a shockwave of good throughout the world that cannot be measured from our mortal vantage point.

God's Gift to You: Creativity and Growth

There is a law of nature that I like to refer to as the Law of Creation, or in scientific circles it's called the "Law of Perpetual Transmutation." It's a law like gravity or centrifugal force. It just is; it simply exists. We can't change it. We can learn to work in harmony with it to be blessed or ignore it at our own risk. This law states that nothing stands still. Everything is either growing or disintegrating. It's either increasing or it's self-destructing.

As a writer, I'm fascinated with the creative process. The more I study and try to develop my creative talents, the more I come to believe that the part of our minds that creates things is the part of us that is made in God's image. Whether it be a book, artwork, a piece of furniture, a poem, a scientific discovery, or a musical piece, we tune into a creative channel (if you will) that enables us to do it. Some tune into the Light of Christ and produce positive works. Others tune into the master of darkness and formulate that which destroys. If you'll notice, Satan never creates anything productive. He only devastates. He takes inventions such as TV, music, radio, the internet and uses them to create despair, despondency and darkness in the world. God, on the other hand, inspires men and women to produce beautiful, positive things and to uplift and enlighten the world with those very same inventions.

John 1:5 tells us that "Jesus is the light that shineth in darkness and the darkness comprehendeth it not." Only those who have a light within them tune into that light, see it, feel it, and channel it to brighten a darkened world.

Whether you think you're creative or not, you were born to be a creator. It is your divine gift! Why do I say that? Because you are made in the image of God. Let's look at Genesis 1:26 again: "And God said, Let us make man in our image, after our likeness: and let them have dominion over the fish of the sea, and over the fowl of the air, and over the cattle, and over all the earth and over every creeping thing that creepeth upon the earth."

There are two things that stand out to me in that verse and the first is that we are made in the image and likeness of God. We have attributes and characteristics that are like Him. The second is that we are made to have dominion over our world. We are free to act for ourselves and not be acted upon. Do you think the Lord meant, "You have dominion over everything but your finances" or "You have dominion over everything but your weight" or "You have dominion over everything but your happiness?" Certainly not!

We are endowed by our Creator with similar creative abilities as He has. Granted they aren't as powerful, but I believe they are more powerful than we realize. To understand our own creative abilities, let's take a look at those of our Creator. The Lord "spoke" the world into existence. He said, "Let there be light and there was light." In John we learn that the Savior was with our Heavenly Father in the beginning – during this creation process. "In the beginning was the Word; and the Word was with God; and the Word was God. The same was in the beginning with God. All things were made by Him; and without Him was not anything made that was made…. And the Word was made flesh and dwelt among us, (and we beheld his glory, the glory as of the only begotten of the Father), full of grace and truth" (John 1:1-14).

God's Word is so powerful that Jesus Christ is referred to as the Word. The Word was "made flesh" or went from a spiritual to a physical form. By God's words the worlds were created. God thought of something and then literally spoke it into existence.

Hebrews 11: 3, 6 says "Through faith we understand that the worlds were framed by the word of God, so that things which are seen were not made of things which do appear." God created the worlds with FAITH. "Faith is the substance of things hoped for and the evidence of things not seen. But without faith it is impossible to please him: for he that cometh to God must believe that he is, and that he is a rewarder of them that diligently seek him."

We too must have faith – not only that He exists, but also that He rewards those who diligently seek after Him! Faith is the literal substance from which God creates our miracles. Without it, nothing happens! Nothing is created! We must not only believe in Him, but also we must believe Him when he says that He will heal our broken hearts and lives. We have to believe Him when He advises us to ask in order to receive and to knock in order to have blessings opened to us.

Spiritual Creation Leads to Physical Creation

Just like our Father in Heaven, we have the ability within us to direct our thoughts, channel our desires and to create them in our physical world. Think about it, the watch on your arm was once a thought in someone's mind. The book you're holding was once only an idea in mine. The house you live in and the chair you sit on both were once only thoughts in someone's mind. Now they have become physical realities.

The person you become is in large measure an outgrowth of your thoughts. Proverbs tells us that as a person thinks in his heart, so is he and that when we commit our works to the Lord, our thoughts will be established (See Proverbs 23:7, 16:3). God, of course, creates on a far grander scale than we, but we still have the ability to turn our thoughts into physical things.

Our words have the ability to create our own world. If we're praying for financial healing, but our words say, "I never have any money." Or "Every time I make a little extra money, something comes along to take it away." Then we are nullifying our prayers. Whatever faith we exercised to start the creative process in motion has just been reversed by our doubting words.

The Critical Nature of Faithfulness

In 1 Chronicles chapter 28 we learn about David and how the Spirit of the Lord gave him a wonderful plan for a temple. David had a great desire to build a temple to God, and he gathered all the things needed – down to the gold for the meat hooks and candlesticks to the laborers to build it. But when it came time to build the temple, the Lord took the privilege away from David because he had not lived worthy of it. He positioned Uriah to be killed in battle. His murder of an innocent man kept him from fulfilling his dream. So he gave the plans and supplies to his son Solomon, and Solomon built the temple instead.

The building of the temple is symbolic of any righteous desire we may have. It starts out in a spiritual way. It's an idea or a desire planted by God in us through the Spirit. Then we start gathering the things we need – the materials, supplies and people we require to achieve it. When all is ready, the righteous desire becomes a physical reality.

But there is an element that must also be present besides the materials, patience to work your plan and allowing it to come to pass in its appointed time. And that is faithfulness. We must never be so arrogant as to think the righteous desires God has given us cannot be fulfilled by another if we do not hold out faithful. David lost the privilege of being the builder of the temple because he did not remain faithful. We must be faithful to God and to the nourishment of our God-given mission in order to bring it to pass.

God has a special plan for each of us – a special mission to fulfill – just like David had a mission to build the temple. Whether we're allowed to complete that mission is entirely up to us. Will we proceed in faith? Will we remain true? Or will we allow ourselves to become sidetracked by the world? Will we give up in fear or doubt?

Like Solomon's temple, every great thing starts as a thought in someone's mind, an idea and gradually starts accumulating what it needs to become a physical reality. That's what Creation is – organizing matter and energy into something new. *You are a creator! More importantly, if you partner with God, you have access to His infinite creative power!*

Are You Growing or Dying?

This same Law of Creation says that "Energy moves into physical form." The image you hold in your mind most often materializes into results in your life. Whatever you give energy to grows. Whatever you give your focus, faith and feeling to increases - whether it's what you want or what you don't want. Worrying is focus and feeling, and when you feed worry you're feeding what you do NOT want! Job, the great sufferer of the Bible, lamented, "For the thing which I greatly feared is come upon me, and that which I was afraid of is come unto me" (Job 3:25).

It takes time for growth to take place. We do not sow and reap at the same time - at least not the same seeds anyway. Many of us after we receive an initial burst of inspiration or righteous desire, proceed a little ways and then reality sets in. We start looking at our surroundings and say, "This is impossible. There's no way." For example, if you have a feeling of peace that the Lord will deliver you from your financial challenges, but then the bill collectors start calling and your bank account is low, the natural thing to do is doubt. But doubt and fear are the worst things you can do because they send your idea back into the nothing. They reverse the creative process.

Paul warned the Hebrews against losing confidence: "Cast not away therefore your confidence, which hath great recompense of reward. For ye have need of patience, that, after ye have done the will of God, ye might receive the promise. Now the just shall live by faith: but if any man draw back, my soul shall have no pleasure in him" (Hebrews 10: 35-38).

2 Timothy 1:7 says: "For God hath not given us the spirit of fear; but of power, and of love, and of a sound mind."

Creation Starts in the Seeds of Thought

In Philippians 4:8 we learn that thoughts are things and are given direction as to the type of thoughts we should dwell upon: "whatsoever things are true, whatsoever things are honest, whatsoever things are just, whatsoever things are pure, whatsoever things are lovely, whatsoever things are of good report; if there be any virtue, and if there be any praise, think on these things."

If we are thinking on these good, lovely and praiseworthy things, do we have time to be worrying? Do we have time to focus on the things we don't want? No! Fill your mind with good things!

Take a hard look at your entertainment and even the
news you watch. Put good things into your mind. As
you do this, you will naturally be propelled forward
toward worthwhile action. True faith elicits action. If
you truly believe a seed will grow and want the
results of the harvest, you will naturally expend the
energy necessary to plant that seed and nourish it
along.

Faith brings what you want to you, but it takes
action to receive it! Just like the growth process of a
seed is not completely within your control, neither is
everything else in your life. You are a co-creator with
God. Your role is to decide which seeds to plant and
to see that they are nourished. But God is in charge of
the miraculous growth process. It is not your role to
supervise or manipulate this creative process. Your
part is simply to retain the vision, stick to your
purpose, and maintain your faith and gratitude.

James Allen in his classic work, *As a Man Thinketh*
explained, "Men imagine that thought can be kept
secret, but it cannot. It rapidly crystallizes into
habit... Thoughts of fear, doubt, and indecision
crystallize into weak, unmanly, and irresolute habits,
which solidify into circumstances of failure,
indigence, and slavish dependence."

YOU CAN'T FLY IF YOU'RE STILL CLUTCHING THE DIRT   31

"Loving and unselfish thoughts crystallize into habits of self-forgetfulness for others, which solidify into circumstances of sure and abiding prosperity and true riches."

"A particular train of thought persisted in, be it good or bad, cannot fail to produce its results on the character and circumstances. A man cannot *directly* choose his circumstances, but he can choose his thoughts, and so indirectly, yet surely, shape his circumstances."

One of my favorite parables of the Savior's is the parable of the talents. I'm sure you know it well. There were three servants and each received a varying number of talents (or coins). The first received five talents, the next two and the third one. The servant who had one talent hid his in the earth because he was afraid. The servants with five and two talents doubled theirs to ten and four respectively. When the master of the servants came, he punished the person who hid his in the ground by taking away his single talent and giving it to the servant who had ten. Then he praised those with ten and four saying, "well done thou good and faithful servant. Thou hast been faithful over a few things, I will make you ruler over many things."

The reason I love this parable is that each time I study it, I learn something new. In the context of our discussion here, let's change those talents or coins to righteous desires. The people who had five and two righteous desires set to work to fulfill those desires. They didn't bury them. They worked toward them with faith and purpose and in the process, they acquired new desires, talents and resources. They became better. They increased – just like everything that God creates is intended to do. But the person who had one and in fear hid his desire and did not seek after it, lost His ability to create. He did not increase. He did not grow, learn or developed. He was in essence "damned" and by that I mean "blocked or stalled in his progression." He couldn't have an increase.

If we're seeking material things so that we may consume them upon our own lusts, for vanity, praise or power, then we are not seeking the kingdom of God. But too many Christians are afraid to dream. They are too afraid to believe that God wants more for them. They think that God wants them to just scrimp by or be content with the bare minimum. Nothing could be further from the truth. God wants you to not only be grateful for what you have, but also grow and develop all of your talents and skills. It may take money, connections and resources for you to do this. It is not wrong for you to accept those things or even ask for them when they are part of a righteous desire. When we seek to build up the kingdom of God, He adds everything we need to get there. We, like the lilies of the field, don't need to worry about where it's going to come from. We simply hold the faith that it will arrive, and in its perfect time it does.

I talk to so many people who have a desire to do wonderful things. They want to help others, lift each other's burdens, and make the world a better place. If you are one of these people, then God gave you that desire! And where there is desire, there is power. Your Heavenly Father isn't cruel. He doesn't give you a desire for something and then not provide a way to accomplish it. Learn God's laws. Learn how He works and together with Him, make those righteous desires a reality.

As Galatians 6:9 says, "let us not be weary in well doing for in due season we shall reap, if we faint not." Faint not, fear not and doubt not, but be believing, for you are laying the foundation of a great work, and out of small and simple things are great things brought to pass.

Christ is the Author and Finisher of Your Faith

In Hebrews 12:2, Christ is referred to as the "author and finisher of our faith." When we put ourselves in His care, His goal is to "finish" - "polish or perfect" our faith. His sole objective is to increase your faith to a level that you can return home to live with Him and your Father in heaven. When we are filled with this faith, we have no room for worry.

As a fiction author, I've gained new insight into the role of our Savior as the author and finisher of our faith. For example, a good author doesn't give you all the facts in the first chapter. He doesn't solve the mystery in chapter one or two. He weaves a tale, holding you in suspense, helping you learn and grow with the characters, come to love the hero or heroine, and then wows you in the end with a wonderful conclusion. He might foreshadow a bit, might give you a foretaste of how it's all going to work out, but He won't reveal the ending completely. That would ruin the story! You might even know how the story will most likely end (happily or the hero reaching his goal) but you don't know HOW just yet. That's how life is. That's how God works.

If we could relax and get to the point where we truly enjoyed the story, resisted flipping to the end to see how it's all going to work out, then we'd enjoy life a whole lot more. So how do you do that? How do you truly relax and live in the NOW? He's already promised us a happy ending if we trust Him in faithfulness! How do you come to truly believe in Him for a happy ending? How do you trust that not only will all things work together for your good, but also you're going to love where He takes you? (Romans 8:28)

I believe the answer lies in discovering the line between what we control and what God controls. Which part of the creative process is ours, and which is His? Every good author eventually addresses the following questions: Who? What? Why? When? Where? and How? In life, there are only two of these questions you can control - the What and the Why. The rest are all up to God. The sooner we release the following questions, the sooner Heavenly Father will open His grip – much like my father did with the bird:

· How is it going to happen?
· When will it occur?
· Who else will be involved in making it happen?
· Where is it going to happen?

Once you release these questions to His care, you'll trust your Heavenly Father, and He'll trust you. You'll have a relationship, and He'll help you fly to your fullest potential. But as long as you struggle and fight over things you can't control, you'll be limited in your sphere of influence and opportunity like a bird trapped in a house.

James Allen in *As a Man Thinketh* put it this way: "As the progressive and evolving being, man is where he is that he may learn that he may grow; and as he learns the spiritual lesson which any circumstance contains for him, it passes away and gives place to other circumstances."

Throughout this book, we'll take an in-depth look at the "Who? What? When? How? Why? and Where?" questions of life and how we can learn to release those elements we can't control and become an active participant in the ones we can. First we'll start with the part of the creation process that God controls. Then we'll examine the "What" and the "Why" questions in which we have a part to play.

Chapter 2: WHO?

"Who?" is actually a question you can control to some degree. You can control yourself. Ultimately YOU are the only person you can control. You have no right to control anyone else.

Thus, for example, it's fruitless for me to try to manipulate you into accomplishing something that I want for you. I have no right to force my will upon you. Likewise, you only have control over yourself. To manipulate a spouse or a friend to get them to do what you want them to do is wrong, and quite frankly, rarely works. Who wants to be manipulated or forced? I don't! Do you? The only exception to this rule might be small children for whom you are responsible to teach and train. Like my father keeping the bird safe, small children do need to be protected. You wouldn't take the time to entice a small child out of the middle of the road. You'd run over there, scoop him up and use whatever force necessary to preserve his life. Yet, even with children in less dangerous circumstances, it's best to lead, guide, and persuade, while keeping force to a minimum.

At first glance you might say, "Well, I only want to control myself. I don't want to dominate or force other people into doing things." I've always said that about myself, yet, there have been times when in the name of "leading someone to the light" I've been tempted and even succumbed to using Satan's tactics. For example, Satan's methods include guilt tripping, pressuring, arguments, contention, sulking, pouting, power struggles, competition, jealousy, manipulation and force.

Let's take a look at several typical times when we're tempted to manipulate others and how we might better handle the situation.

Spiritual Relationships

Paul admonished "Be not unequally yoked together with unbelievers: for what fellowship hath righteousness with unrighteousness? And what communion hath light with darkness?" (2 Corinthians 6:14) Yet, there are many times in life where the ideal is simply not realistic. You could already be in a friendship or marriage relationship with an unbeliever before you become a believer yourself. Or you may have family who are not believers. Other times, you may have a spouse, friends, or family members who believe, but they aren't quite as consistently obedient as you, or perhaps they have slipped into complete rebellion. There are a myriad of reasons why in a day-to-day environment you will encounter those who may not be on the same spiritual plane as you.

We shouldn't shun others who do not believe as we do. Rather we should be there to lift, serve and love them. Inherent in these situations are times of frustration when the person you care for is not reaching their full potential. They aren't seeing the possibilities that you see for them.

Probably the hardest challenge in letting go is when our goals, plans, and dreams involve other people and their ability to grow on a spiritual level. When your future is tied to someone else, and he or she is unwilling or lacks the vision or courage to go where you want to go, what can you do? Do you halt your development and progression to wait on this other person to catch up? Do you run on and leave them behind? Or is there some other happy medium? You can't force someone else to see your vision, to follow your path. Arguing and pressuring only serve to drive them to dig in their heels, or worse, run in the opposite direction.

When we think of how God leads us in our lives, we find the answer. Firmness, not force is the key. God never gives in or wavers in His course, but He is longsuffering and ever-willing to take us back. We, as He, must be firm in our convictions, steadfast, focused and committed. Leading others up the path of truth requires love, patience, gentleness, diligence, meekness — and yes, time.

How many times have we messed up and Jesus is still there waiting and willing — standing at the door and knocking if we will but let Him in? He never beats the door down. He never even picks the lock and sneaks in through manipulation. He doesn't shout, belittle or guilt-trip us from the other side of the door. He simply patiently stands there and knocks until the time arrives that we have the ears to hear the knocking and the willingness and courage to open the door.

Jesus knows that force, manipulation, power games, and dominion will never lead someone else to the light. Love, service, patient teaching and a good example will do more to soften hearts and shape lives than any argument or debate. Do you have a loved one who is choosing the wrong paths? Are they digging in their heels when you would really like them to join you on your walk up the path of truth?

Then, follow Christ's example. Be His partner in this endeavor. Be an instrument in His hands to help your friend or loved one hear the knocking. Take the time to teach them to listen and hear the tapping. When the time is right for them, take their hand and walk with them to open the door through which more joy and happiness than they ever dreamed possible exists.

The beautiful thing about this process is that as we strain to hear Christ at the door for our friend's sake, we hear Him ourselves. As we take our friend's hand to walk with them to the door, we can't help but arrive there ourselves. And when our friend opens the door, we will be there to feel the flood of joy and happiness that flows as Christ enters.

Romantic Relationships

The most common advice request that comes in through SheLovesGod.com is romantic in nature. Generally, the woman writing wants to get married, and she's set her heart on one man in particular. Often, she's prayed and feels as if she's received a confirmation that this man is "the one." Now, how to make him realize that? What if he never sees it for himself? What should she do now?

Let's go back to our rule: You cannot control anyone but yourself. Everyone else is beyond your control, and you have no right to manipulate them or force them to see or do things your way. You are free to love, lift, inspire and serve. These you may do freely. But when you seek to force your will upon another through manipulation, mind games, or force, you're stepping over the line. Cross the line, and you do so at your own peril! Frustration, anxiety and even a complete destruction of the relationship could result.

Rest assured that if this man is truly "the one," he will come to know it for himself. This kind of revelation comes in pairs. God will not reveal a marriage partnership to one person and deny it to the other, but the timing of that revelation is in God's hands. "When" is a question only God can control. If you are in such a situation, then remember what you can do – love, serve, lift and inspire. Most of all, be patient! But do it all purely and without ulterior motive. If you act out of manipulation or game playing, you're traveling a risky path.

Later in the chapter on "What?" I'll explain how to get clear on what you want through visualization, goal setting and gratitude. If you choose to use these tools in a romantic relationship – avoid putting a name or a face on the vision or goal. It is perfectly fine to say, "I am so happy and grateful that I am married to a man who is romantic, fun, communicative, loving and who encourages and allows me to reach my full potential." It is not okay to say, "I am so happy and grateful that I am married to Fred Jones because he is romantic, fun, communicative, etc."

Leave Fred Jones out of it. You have no right to make a WHO a WHAT. He has his own volition. He's not an object for you to obtain or manipulate! Trust the Lord that if Fred chooses not to be a part of your life that God will lead you to someone even more suitable.

Business Relationships

In business, you'll often need to form relationships or alliances with other people to reach your goals. For example, a network marketer needs people for his or her team who are self-motivated, hard working, visionary and coachable. Like the romantic example, you may set specific targets for the type of people you want on your team, but you have no right to make specific people the "What" of your goal.

For example, it is helpful to write, "I am so happy and grateful that self-motivated, hard-working, visionary and coachable individuals are continually brought to my business team, and together we achieve [specific goals here]."

It is not proper to write, "I am so happy and grateful that Sam Jones, Mary Smith and Frank Bennett are on my team and are reaching [specific levels] because they are self-motivated, hard-working, visionary and coachable."

Even if you feel it's in their best interest, you have no right to set goals for someone else. Let them do that for themselves! Also, you'll experience less stress if you'll keep any goal that involves relationships impersonal – whether they be romantic, business, spiritual, friendships, or familial. You'll be less likely to meddle in another person's affairs, less worried over their immediate progress, and free to find better relationships that are more ideally suited if need be.

When we let go of our need to control other people, we release an immense amount of frustration, and we liberate the other person to more easily reach their potential. I have one friend in particular who I worked with quite intensely for a couple years on a spiritual level. This person made great strides and learned many new and wonderful things, yet she was still unable to fully commit to a spiritual course. It became very frustrating for me because obviously she wanted to reach a certain spiritual destination, but she let fear stand in her way. There's nothing quite so heartbreaking as watching someone you love deny themselves blessings just because they're scared to take a leap of faith – a leap you've taken and discovered that, for you, it wasn't such a leap after all.

Unfortunately, I must admit that I used many of Satan's tactics – guilt trips, manipulation and pressure. I allowed myself to become frustrated and even angry at times. Did this do any good? Of course not! If anything, it slowed her progress because she sensed my frustration and anxiety. No one wants to be forced and pressured!

In this particular incident, the Lord gave me a very clear answer that He had my friend within His care, and that she would be all right. She would reach her desired destination eventually. But, it wasn't my job to meddle in how or when she reached it. All of that was between her and her Father in Heaven.

When I finally relinquished everything but the vision He'd given me – the assurance that He'd given me that all would be well in the end – an immense burden lifted from my shoulders. I then realized it was never my responsibility to figure out the right words to say or the correct things to do to convince my friend to take a leap of faith. My job was simply to love, lift, serve and believe in her!

An amazing thing happened when I let go of my need to control. She made such an amazing amount of progress without me bugging her! She and the Lord did just fine on their own. In this particular incident, the Lord had given me a vision of the Who and the What, but I had to relinquish the When and the How!

Points to Ponder

· How does it make you feel when people try to manipulate or control you? How do you react?
· How have you sought to control other people, even in small ways, in the past?
· How will you let go of your need to control, manipulate or force others in the future?
· What will you do when other people disappoint you or let you down?

Chapter 3: When?

Ten minutes before *Bob the Builder* is to start, four-year-old Nate enters my office, "Mom, change it to Nick Jr."

"Just a minute, Nate, let me finish this one thing."

"But it's taking soooo looonngg. Why is it taking so long?"

"You just asked me Nate, plus it's not time for *Bob the Builder* yet."

"But it's taking soooo looonngg. Why is it taking soooo long?"

"Ask me right, Nate, you're not asking me the right way."

"Please, will you turn on Nick Jr?"

I rise from my desk and turn the TV onto Nick Jr. Of course, it's not time for *Bob the Builder* to start yet. A couple minutes later, Nate enters my office again.

"Mom, change it to Nick Jr."

"I just did, Nate"

"Change it to Nick Jr."

"Ask me right, Nate, you're not asking me the right way."

"Please, will you change it to Nick Jr?"

I go to the living room and see that in his impatience, Nate has changed the channel. I flip it back onto Nick Jr. and *Bob the Builder's* theme song is playing, "Bob the Builder, can he fix it? Yes he can!"

All is right in Nate's world....at least for the next 30 minutes.

I've caught myself many times approaching my Heavenly Father in a similar attitude as Nate.

"Please, Heavenly Father, help me with this problem."

"Wait just a little while until My timing is right."

"But it's taking soooo looonngg. Why is it taking so long?"

"Be patient... I've got it covered."

"But it's taking soooo looonngg! Why is it taking so long? I think if I just did this and that, I could fix the situation myself."

"Be patient, it will all work out. I promise."

"Heavenly Father, everything's a mess now. Why won't you help me? Why can't I just get past this problem?"

"Child, please trust me."

"I'm sorry, You've done so much for me. I'm so sorry for my ingratitude. Thank you for my many blessings. Thank you for your patience. I will trust You to deliver me from this problem when Your timing is perfect."

"That's my girl... There you go. The problem's solved."

"Thank You so much! There I was fretting, and You had it covered all the time! Your timing is always perfect!"

"You're welcome," He says and then adds with a twinkle in His eye, "You might want to remember that the next time."

Live in the Now

Ecclesiastes 3:1 says "To every thing there is a season, and a time to every purpose under the heaven."

Are you like me? Do you get frustrated waiting for the things you want? Most of us despise waiting, and it's primarily because we have some goal out in front of us that we want to reach, and we want to reach it **right now**.

Something that happened to our family during a family trip is a good illustration. One autumn, my husband Greg and I took our six children to Gatlinburg, Tennessee in the Smokey Mountains for the day. It's about a 2.5 hour drive there and a 2.5 hour drive back. We got up around 4:00 a.m., loaded up the kids and were off by 4:45 a.m. We arrived at our favorite pancake house around 7:30 a.m. My

husband always likes to arrive early. As a matter of
fact, we were so early, that when we finished eating,
none of the shops were open and it drizzled outside.
So we went into a little mountain mall to kill time.
Maybe two shops in the entire mall were open then,
so we passed the hours letting the kids ride up and
down the elevator or the escalators or having races to
see who could beat the elevator down the stairs.

Finally the stores opened, and we window
shopped until about noon. Then, my husband
informed us that it was time to go to Cades Cove – a
scenic drive up into the mountains to a primitive little
village. I've been to Gatlinburg and Cades Cove so
many times, it really didn't matter much to me where
we went or what we did.

So we set off on an hour drive to Cades Cove
through the beautiful Smokey Mountains. It hadn't
been cold enough for the leaves to change much, but
it was still beautiful to see the subtle yellows, oranges
and greens and the rocky river winding along either
side of us as we listened to inspiring music.

Cades Cove is a park with a six mile loop that
passes through a few cabins, but mainly it's forest
and meadows. There's also a mill at about the
halfway point where you can park and walk around.

It took us literally two hours to creep along bumper-to-bumper through this six mile loop. After about an hour or so of this, my husband started to lose his temper. Couldn't people read the signs that say "Be polite, no stopping, keep the traffic moving?" Evidently not. They stopped for every squirrel or deer they encountered. Drivers hung out their car windows to take pictures.

My husband and I have an unspoken system. If he loses it, I must remain calm. If I lose it, he remains calm. So as he began to lose it, I rallied the children into a series of games to keep them occupied – everybody name a place that starts with A, then B, then C and so on. We invented imaginary worlds – each person describing some element of it. The time passed rather painlessly - for us anyway. But because the traffic was so bad, my husband didn't even stop at the mill. We just kept on driving so we could get back in time for dinner.

Finally, we were out of the cove, traffic moving at a good clip, and we hit another bottleneck and spent 30 minutes going eight-tenths of a mile. This time, even I became impatient, because when the traffic started rolling, having had no lunch, we had all begun to anticipate dinner. I also became increasingly aware of the fact that our recently potty-trained toddler hadn't had a bathroom break in hours! It was after 5:00 P.M. before we reached the restaurant and nearly 6:00 P.M. before we sat down to our delicious meal.

But do you know what? Those children didn't complain once! Ten hours total in the car all day, and they didn't gripe or complain one time about it! With six kids, you don't go a lot of places and they were grateful just to be taken somewhere. It was all new to at least four of the children who had never spent any time in Gatlinburg. Even riding in the car couldn't put a damper on that for them.

The only person who didn't enjoy the trip was Greg. He was too irritated to join in the games. For him the trip was a disappointment, but for the rest of us who used the waiting time to bond and enjoy the scenery and listen to music, we had a pleasant time. Now, I'm not saying I'm better than my husband in this regard. We just have that unspoken rule, and he claimed "irritated" first and tenaciously hung onto it so I had to claim "make the best of it." Maybe someday we'll learn to "make the best of it" simultaneously.

Why do I share this story? Because we spend way too much of our lives waiting for what we want to happen. Of all the questions we wish we could control, I think WHEN is probably the one we covet most. We want things and we want them NOW. We can't wait until graduation, can't wait to marry, can't wait to have our first child, can't wait to get the kids out of the house, can't wait to retire, and then what do we have left? Death? We've just wished our lives away!

When will we learn to live in the NOW? Now is really all you have. Yesterday is gone and certainly cannot be changed. Tomorrow isn't here yet. Now is all you have. Most of the time, if you look at this moment you're in, you'll see that things are just fine right now. Right now as I write this, I'm listening to some beautiful uplifting music; I've just had a delicious breakfast so I'm well fed. The words are flowing, my computer is working. I have everything I need in this moment.

It's when we start worrying about later in the day or tomorrow or the next week, month or year that we start envisioning problems. If we'd let go of our worries over tomorrow and guilt over yesterday and focus on the moment, we'd see that God has given us everything we need in this moment. For years, I wondered what Christ meant by "sufficient is the day unto the evil thereof" (Matthew 6:34), then

finally I understood. The Lord provides everything
you need today to deal with whatever part or portion
of your challenges that must be dealt with today.
Today may not hold tomorrow's answers, but it holds
today's!

Another law of nature known as the law of
gestation or the law of the harvest states that every
seed has a gestation or incubation period. If you look
at a packet of bean seeds, you'll see they take a few
months to grow. A baby takes about 40 weeks inside
its mother. A fruit tree takes about three years to bear
fruit. God has placed around us in nature constant
reminders of the fact that everything has a set period
of time to grow and bear fruit.

He's trying to teach us that just as natural seeds
have germination periods, so do spiritual seeds. Ideas
are spiritual seeds and will move into form or
physical results provided they are given the
nourishment they need. Your goals will manifest in
their perfect time. Just as it takes time for water to
crystallize into ice, and just as it takes some time for
an acorn to become a tree or a bean seed to become a
bean plant and grow more beans, so it takes time for
your ideas to germinate and become physical
realities.

Every idea seed has its own gestation period... the time it takes to grow. Unfortunately, there's no packet to read to find out how long it's going to take. But just as physicals seeds grow faster with proper nourishment and rich soil, so do spiritual seeds. Your level of faith and diligence can speed up or slow down the process. But, generally there's going to be a certain time frame that must transpire before it becomes tangible.

Give your idea seeds time to grow. Don't rip them out of the ground in doubt or unbelief. Remember, you don't sow and reap at the same time. The nourishment you give your idea seeds is diligence, purpose, faith and patience. If you want to kill your ideas, feed them doubt, fear and negativity.

When I learned this principle, it was like a light bulb went on inside me. I could look back at any achievement and see that it took time to grow and that it eventually did take shape – even if it took months or even years.

Ecclesiastes 3:17 tells us that *"there is* a time for every purpose and for every work." Trust that the inspiration you receive today will become a reality when the time for it arrives.

The Lord's Timing Is Best

Time and again, the Lord has taught me that His timing is best. It may seem like things aren't going to work out in time or that things aren't going your way, but if you'll trust His perfect timing, it will all fall into place.

One example of this was when my husband and I needed to get a bigger house for our growing family. Pay close attention to this story as I share it, for it is a good example of which Who? What? When? Why? Where? And How? questions we can control.

From 1995 – 1996, my sister Karen, her husband Glenn, my parents, Greg and I decided we wanted to get a large parcel of property and build homes on it. We had very specific criteria for what we wanted. My dad wanted a water source – either a creek or a pond. My sister and I wanted to be close enough to civilization that we could access things we needed for our home businesses. Finally, we all wanted to be far enough from the city to be isolated and away from city lights and noisy neighbors.

We designated my sister Karen to look for the property. "Please help Aunt KK find our property" became a regular part of our family prayers. I can still hear my little ones praying this. By December of 1996, we still hadn't found anything. Greg and I now had four children in a 1,100 square foot house. We were anxious for something bigger!

I'm not one to read a newspaper. I don't even care to watch television news, but one Thursday in December as I passed a newspaper my husband left on the kitchen table, something told me to pick it up and look in the land section. I opened it and found that the 100 acre Battlefield Stables by the Chickamauga Battlefield in Georgia was to be auctioned off on Saturday.

I had a distinctive feeling about this ad, that it could be what we were looking for. We knew we didn't have enough money for 100 acres. We were looking for something more along the lines of 25 acres, but something told me to check into it. I immediately called my father and spoke to him about it. I asked if he'd go with me to look at the property. He said he would, but recommended that I not get my hopes up. Odds were it cost more than we could afford.

We drove to Georgia that afternoon. Interestingly enough, we'd never looked in Georgia for property. We thought we should stay in Tennessee. But back to

the story… it had been raining and the weather was
chilly. My father spoke to a man at the stables, got a
map of the property and found that they were
auctioning it off in tracts. We wouldn't be required to
buy it all. My dad looked at the map and decided
he'd like to look at the back 24 acres. I had the baby
with me, so I stayed in the car and waited for him to
trek back there.

I still remember waiting with Jillian who was only
a month old, hoping and praying that this would be
the answer to our prayers. I felt hopeful, but even if
my dad came back with a positive report, would we
be able to win the auction?

When my dad returned to his station wagon, he
was so excited. This was the place! It had a creek
surrounding two sides of the property. It had a hill
overlooking a beautiful open meadow. It was only 10
minutes away from major stores, only 20 minutes
from Chattanooga, Tennessee, yet was completely
isolated. It had everything we wanted!

We went back home and told Greg and my sister
and brother-in-law about it. My brother-in-law,
Glenn, was hesitant. He actually considered moving
his family to Pennsylvania with his job and didn't
think now would be the time to buy a piece of

property. Neither he nor my sister was incredibly thrilled with the idea of moving to Georgia. With a little coaxing, Glenn, Karen, my dad, Greg and I attended the auction on Saturday morning. Before the auction, we walked back to the 24 acre plot. As we came into the clearing, there was an audible sigh from each of us. We looked toward the hill and could picture our houses there. We just knew that this was our property! It would require building a half-mile road to reach it, but my dad had a bulldozer and knew how to use it.

We agreed unanimously that we wanted it and went back to sit down in the folding chairs under the auction tent. We watched the other plots go for $5,000 an acre. We knew we couldn't afford $5,000 an acre for 24 acres! We weren't even sure where we'd get the money for it at a lower price. Greg and I had saved some money, but it wasn't enough. My dad said he could talk to my uncle about getting some cash for my part of the inheritance on my grandfather's estate that was still in probate. But we couldn't be certain we'd get it.

Whatever we bought that day would have to be paid in full within a week. My sister had more money saved than we did, so if we won the property she could put down the deposit.

We sat there in one of the back rows observing attentively as these plots went for twice what we could afford. We decided we could pay perhaps $2,500 per acre at most. We designated one of us as the bidder. When the plot came up for auction, I had nervous knots twirling in my stomach, and my heart thumped in anticipation.

We had a few people bid against us, but not as many as the other tracts – probably because this tract didn't touch the road and would require the expense of building our own. We ended up winning the auction for $2,400 per acre! We were so excited, but we still weren't sure how we'd come up with the money within a week. My dad talked with my uncle and got my share of the inheritance in cash whereas normally it would have taken years. My sister finagled her finances and got her part, and my Dad worked his magic to find his share. We bought the property, and my dad set to work building the road.

For us, it was nothing short of a miracle. Through this experience I learned three important lessons:

·   Get a clear picture of what you want and ask specifically. We knew what we were looking for in our property, and we asked the Lord persistently for it.

·   Don't worry about how it's going to happen. But
    most definitely, listen to the still small voice when
    it prompts you! If I hadn't picked up that
    newspaper, we wouldn't have found our
    property.

·   When you find what you want, grab it and trust
    that the Lord will provide a way. We weren't sure
    how we would come up with the money. We just
    trusted that the Lord would open the door. He
    did!

I designed our house plan. We found a reasonable
builder and started construction on our new home in
September of 1997. Karen and Glenn started theirs
about the same time. We made some repairs on our
home and put it up for sale, but it didn't sell. Our
new home was scheduled for completion, and we still
didn't have a buyer by February. I started sweating
bullets and checked into ways we could possibly rent
our current house and live in the new one. Our credit
was bad because of a debt consolidation we'd done in
1991, so we would need a FHA loan. Because FHA
would only finance up to about $95,000, we'd have
to come up with the rest in cash. How were we going
to do that?

We had some money saved, but not the $21,000 we needed. Even with the sale of the old house, coming up with that much would have been extremely difficult. Finally when the realtor contract was up, our new home still wasn't done because of all the rains we'd had that winter. That bought us a little time. I went to the store and bought a kit on how to sell your own home. I found a local mortgage company who would finance our existing house for 100% financing for the new buyer and had them print a flyer for me on what the new buyer would pay per month to live in the house.

Then I ran a "for sale by owner" ad in the local paper, and dropped the sale price down so that the realtor commission wasn't on it. It was a steal of a deal, and I gave anyone who came to look at the house the flyer from the mortgage company so they would know exactly what it would take to get into the home.

We had a buyer within a couple weeks. Because our new house wasn't done, we actually closed on the old house before the new one completed. Because of builder delays, we had to be out of the old house before the financing could be arranged on the new one. The builder let us move into the new house and pay him rent until the financing finalized. By the time we closed, two months later, our credit history had improved enough that we were able to get a regular loan. We weren't bound by the FHA limitation and were able to get into the house for the amount of money we had saved!

I learned from this experience that God's timing is perfect! He knows what He is doing. All the worrying and attempting to manipulate the situation to get the house to sell sooner – if it had worked – would not have been the best timing. We wouldn't have had enough money for the house. And the way it worked out, our old house was perfect for the nice young couple who purchased it.

"For the vision is yet for an appointed time, but at the end it shall speak, and not lie: though it tarry, wait for it; because it will surely come, it will not be late."
(Habbakuk 2:3)

"Humble yourselves therefore under the mighty hand of God, that He may exalt you in due time."
(1 Peter 5:6)

"I will therefore that men pray everywhere, lifting up holy hands, without wrath and doubting."
(1 Timothy 2:8)

To Everything There Is a Season

Along with understanding that God has a perfect
time for everything is knowing that there is a season
for each part of our lives.

Ecclesiastes 3:1-8 says,

*"To every thing there is a season, and a time to every
purpose under the heaven:*
*A time to be born, and a time to die; a time to plant,
and a time to pluck up that which is planted;*
*A time to kill, and a time to heal; a time to break
down, and a time to build up;*
*A time to weep, and a time to laugh; a time to mourn,
and a time to dance;*
*A time to cast away stones, and a time to gather
stones together; a time to embrace, and a time to refrain
from embracing;*
*A time to get, and a time to lose; a time to keep, and a
time to cast away;*
*A time to rend, and a time to sew; a time to keep
silence, and a time to speak;*
*A time to love, and a time to hate; a time of war, and
a time of peace."*

All around us in nature, God illustrates that there is a rhythm to life. Some examples of this include the tide as it goes in and out, night following day, and seasons changing. We have cycles ourselves – cycles in our bodies and with our moods. I have noticed a pattern in my own temperament where I go through a creative phase, followed by a productive phase and then a few days of heavy organization. I've learned to recognize these moods and work with them. I don't try to write a fiction story when I'm in a production mode. If I wait for the creative mode to roll back around, the story will flow in half the time. Instead of forcing the creative process in the productive phase, I do my bookkeeping or general maintenance on my web sites.

There's a natural flow to life. When hard times hit, remember that good times are coming. They must — just as dawn follows the darkness.

Enjoy the Journey

The Apostle Paul explained, "for I have learned, in whatsoever state I am, therewith to be content. I know both how to be abased, and I know how to abound: every where and in all things I am instructed both to be full and to be hungry, both to abound and

to suffer need. I can do all things through Christ
which strengtheneth me" (Philippians 4:11-13).

Over the last few years, I feel as if God has been
teaching me to "Enjoy the journey!" He's brought
some wonderful people into my life to model this
principle. They've taught me that happiness and
hardship are not mutually exclusive. One of these
people lives local to me and the other lives across the
country. Each of them struggle with their own
difficult challenges, yet each manages to find the
cheerful, the humorous and the fun in everyday
living. Together they've taught me to lighten up and
enjoy life – even when things don't appear to be
going my way.

Also, with the opportunity to delve into fiction,
I've learned to enjoy the lighter side of life and not
take things so seriously. It's helped me see my life
from an author's perspective. As I watch things start
to come together for our family, I see the master
genius in the works and designs of a kind, wise,
loving Heavenly Father and of our atoning Savior
Jesus Christ who is the "author and finisher of our
faith." (Hebrews 12:2). He's an author who always
provides a happy ending if we see our existence on
an eternal canvas.

Think of your life as a compelling novel. If you truly believed in a happy ending – KNEW it would come – then you could relax and enjoy the story, letting it unfold before your eyes. You'd enjoy the journey and appreciate all the little nuances and symbolism along the way.

Too many of us are "human doings" instead of "human beings." We rush to the "event points" in the saga of our lives. We want to hurry to the moments when the house is sold, the new one built, the wedding day, the birth, the new job, the mortgage paid in full. We let ourselves remain anxious, frustrated, and worried in between. We waste the waiting period. But really, it's not a waiting period. It's your life! Those day to day moments between where you are and where you want to be are your life! They are the NOW moments. And NOW is really all you have. Everything happens in the NOW. Our Heavenly Father wants us to learn to enjoy the moment we're in, to be grateful for it, and to make the best of it, as we remain ever grateful and faithful for "good things to come" (Hebrews 9:11).

God is a master author who knows how to weave a story that carries you along, spellbinds, mystifies and offers a magnificent happy ending. But for Him, there really is no end… it's the story that never

ends... thanks to our Savior and Redeemer who died
on the cross and rose the third day that we might live
forever in His presence.

When I finally let go of the questions I couldn't
control and decided that I knew absolutely for certain
that God would make it all work out in the end –
even better than I could imagine it happening - it all
started falling into place. I have no delusions that my
faith is perfect or that it can't grow more. The story
isn't fully told, and I'm glad it isn't! I'm enjoying the
journey and gratefully watching His masterpiece
develop before my eyes.

Don't Compare Yourself with Others

There is another law of nature known as the Law
of Relativity that states that things just are. We make
them big, small, easy or difficult by how we look at
them. If I were to draw a circle on a piece of paper
the size of a quarter and asked you if it was a large or
small circle, you might look at me funny, unsure of
how to answer. But if I drew a circle the size of a
dime next it and then asked you if the quarter-size
circle was large or small, then you would say it was
large. But if I then proceeded to show you a circle the
size of an entire sheet of notebook paper, you'd say,
"oh, that quarter-size circle is small."

You can't tell if anything is large or small until you compare it to something else. It's the comparison that gives it its characteristics. Rich is relative. You may think someone who makes $200,000 per year is rich. But if you compare him to someone who makes $5 million per year, he doesn't look so rich anymore.

Most of us use this law against ourselves. We take our weaknesses and compare ourselves to other people's strengths. We say, "I'll never be able to sew as well as Christy." Or "My house would never stay as organized and as clean as Jane's." Or we may try to puff ourselves up by saying, "Look at Mary, her house is a wreck. She needs to be more like me."

We don't need to use this law against ourselves – we don't need to be comparing our worsts with another's bests. Nor do we need to be puffing ourselves up with pride by comparing our bests with another's worsts. We also don't need to compare the Lord's time table for our lives with the one that belongs to someone else.

The way we can use this law to our benefit is to realize that other people can look at the same situation and see it totally differently than we do. They come from a different frame of reference. It can help us understand other people better. If I tell you

something is "expensive" – well compared to what?
Don't limit yourself by your perspective on things.
What you think may be "hard or difficult" would be
a piece of cake for the Lord.

Have you ever felt assured in those sweet hours of
prayer that the Lord has promised you a blessing?
Perhaps you've felt the comforting peace that you
would receive deliverance from a challenge or that a
loved one will one day return to God. But then time
passes and nothing happens and you begin to
wonder and doubt. So much time may even pass that
it now seems impossible that you could receive the
promise. It seems too late, perhaps you feel too old,
too inadequate, or the problem has magnified with
the waiting. Notice all of these are relative terms – too
late, too old, too inadequate compared to what?

In Genesis the Lord promised Abraham that he
would make him a great nation and that his children
would be as numerous as the sands of the sea and the
stars in the sky. God promised Abraham this at a
time when it certainly seemed possible. He was a
young man in love with his wife Sarah. But years
passed, and Abraham and Sarah tried with no
success to have a child. By the time the Lord and
three messengers came to visit them, Genesis 18:11
says that Sarah had become "old and well stricken in

age, and it ceased to be with Sarah after the manner of women." If anyone had a reason to use the law of relativity against themselves, it was Abraham and Sarah!

Upon this visit the Lord assured Abraham once more, "I will certainly return unto thee according to the time of life; and, lo, Sarah thy wife shall have a son."

Sarah, who stood by the tent door as Abraham sat with the messengers, overheard their conversation and laughed within herself, saying "After I am waxed old shall I have pleasure, my lord being old also?"

And the Lord said to Abraham, "Wherefore did Sarah laugh saying, 'Shall I of a surety bear a child, which am old?' Is any thing too hard for the Lord? At the time appointed I will return unto thee, according to the time of life, and Sarah shall have a son."

According to the word of the Lord, "Sarah conceived, and bare Abraham a son in his old age, **at the set time** of which God had spoken to him" (Genesis 21:2). Abraham was 100 years old when Isaac was born to Sarah.

The poignant question, "Is anything too hard for the Lord?" was answered with a resplendent and eternal "NO!" Nothing is too hard for the Lord! A large majority of people who walk this earth are the descendants of father Abraham and mother Sarah. Their grandson Jacob had twelve sons who became the twelve tribes of Israel and those tribes are scattered about the world. Most of us could probably claim lineage through one of them. Abraham's children did become as numerous as the stars of the sky and the sands of the seashore!

This scriptural account demonstrates many of the fundamental principles we've discussed.

First, when the Lord makes a promise, He keeps it. It doesn't matter how impossible or challenging it may seem to us, we may rest assured that the Lord can make anything happen. "For with God, nothing shall be impossible" (Luke 1:37).

When we compare our situation to the Lord's perspective, there's nothing too deep, too hard, too overwhelming, or too difficult that He can't fix. Problems, challenges, talents, and abilities will vary from person to person. You can always find someone who is better or worse than you at any given thing, but God is better than us all at everything. There is nothing "bad" in Him. There is only the "good." God is bigger than it all.

When we ask in faith according to God's will, He promises to grant our petitions. In 1 John 5:14-15 we read, "And this is the confidence that we have in him, that, if we ask any thing **according to his will**, he hears us: And if we know that he hears us, whatsoever we ask, we know that **we have** the petitions that we desired of him."

Notice that we *have them*! It doesn't say *we might have them* or we *will have them.* It says we already have them! They are ours, already promised and now it's just a matter of time for them to be delivered. It's like ordering some products from your favorite mail order company. They're yours, you've bought them. They're on their way. It's just a matter of time to receive the delivery. We can trust that God is infinitely more reliable than any mail order company or postal carrier! He delivers even on weekends, national holidays and during rain, sleet, snow and hail or even when your neighbor is parked in front of your mail box!

The second lesson in this story is that God has appointed times for events. Notice that the account says that Sarah conceived and bore Abraham a son "at the set time." God has set an appointment on His calendar for the delivery of your promised blessings. To attempt to change that time will only lead to frustration and unnecessary worry and doubt. In reality, if we comprehended all that the Lord comprehends, we would not wish to alter His perfect timing. To do so may result in an incomplete blessing or missing out on some portion of it that makes it truly wondrous and full. In God's perfect timing and perfect way, He usually helps others while He fulfills your blessing. He never helps only one when he can help two, three or a multitude more!

Third, appearances are not truth. We must admit that we do not comprehend all that the Lord comprehends. Just because appearances suggest that the promise will not be delivered, it matters very little. The Lord is the champion of lost causes. He loves to produce miracles in the lives of His followers. Faith is to think truth regardless of appearances. FEAR is False Evidence Appearing Real.

Fear is looking at things through distorted eyes. Faith, on the other hand, knows the truth - that the seed lies beneath the soil swelling and sprouting, even if the plant with the fruit isn't visible yet. No matter how bad things get or impossible they appear, if the Lord has promised, then He has promised. Whether it is delivered in this life or in the eternities, it will be delivered.

In summary, the principles we've discussed in this chapter are:

· **Enjoy the journey.** Make the best of wherever you are. And if it's bad, know that good times are coming.

· **Know that every idea has a gestation period.** Give it time to grow. Feed it faith, and diligently work toward it in gratitude.

· **When you feel like you've been banished to a waiting room, use that time to grow closer to God.** He's probably trying to teach you something. And if you take that time to grow closer to Him through prayer, asking questions, and scripture study, He'll be able to give you the answers you need.

Look for the spiritual lessons in your trials and in those times when life seems to drag along. Don't waste the wait, look for the spiritual lessons that God scatters all along your path. Just like our drive through Cades Cove… His beauty surrounded us, but when we were too aggravated about the slow traffic, we couldn't see it nor did we care about it. Learn to enjoy God's beauty. Be grateful for the moment while you're in it. Don't wait until you look back on it or worse never appreciate it at all.

Points to Ponder

- Can you think of prior times when you thought things were taking too long, but everything worked out at the perfect time?
- How have you "wasted the wait" in the past?
- If you are currently in a waiting mode, what are some things you can be doing now to creatively make use of this time?
- How can you "be still" and gratefully know that your Heavenly Father is God and is working everything together for your good - even in times when it seems He's taking too long?
- While you're waiting, count your blessings. What do you have right now that you are grateful for?
- Have you prayed and received a positive confirmation for the things you seek? Have you documented this answer in writing and read and reread it?
- If you're starting to lose faith, how much time are you spending gratefully visualizing the outcome the Lord has promised?

Chapter 4: How?

I want to get out of debt, but how? I want a new car, but how will I afford it? I want to get married, but how am I going to meet the right person? I want a bigger home, but how will we obtain it? Do you find yourself asking questions like these? You know what you want, but you have no idea how you're going to achieve or obtain it.

When I think of the "How" question, I think of the parable of the acorn. Think about an acorn. Within it lies the blueprint for a full grown oak tree. But it isn't an oak yet. It's just the plan. It must be planted in the right type of soil, nourished and given time to grow into its ultimate creation.

Notice that the acorn only gathers what it needs as it needs it. It doesn't collect bark while it's sprouting from a seed, and it doesn't worry about going out and finding leaf elements while it's small. It has the vision or blueprint for its ultimate objective – an oak tree – but it doesn't know when or how the things it needs will come to it. It doesn't go out and fight and claw to get what it wants. It doesn't need to steal anything from anyone else. Everything it needs comes to it. We need to be like the acorn and trust the vision and take action on our current environment.

What if an acorn said, "Why try? I have no idea where I'm going to get that bark. Where am I going to get those leaves? I'm just a seed! I'm too small!" Yet, this is exactly how we're prone to think. "I can't make a big difference in the world; I'm just one little person with few talents or skills." Or "I want to write a book, but I'll probably never find a publisher, so why try?" Or "I have an idea for a revolutionary invention, but why make it when I can't afford to have it manufactured and marketed?"

When we think or say things like this, we're not taking into account that God will give us everything in our immediate environment that we need when we need it – just like He does for the acorn. "Consider the lilies of the field, how they grow; they toil not, neither do they spin: And yet I say unto you, That even Solomon in all his glory was not arrayed like one of these" (Matthew 6:28-29). If the things we need are not readily available, He'll bring them to us! If there is no way in sight, He'll open a way.

I cannot tell you how many times the Lord has brought someone into my life from clear across the country to bring me the skills or the resources I needed next. One instance in particular comes to mind.

There's a door that I'd been beating on for nearly a decade that refused to open for me. I wanted to write a book that would be sold on the shelves of one particular bookstore chain. Over the years, I've submitted manuscripts to this chain's publishing house, only to receive rejection letters. Then I self-published and sent my books to this company, but the door remained sealed.

Over a decade I continued to write on a consistent basis. When I couldn't find a publisher to take on my work, I learned how to do the technical part of publishing for myself. When the bookstores wouldn't give me shelf space, I used virtual shelf space on my own web sites, Amazon and the web sites of major bookstores. All the while I kept knocking on the door of this one particular bookstore chain.

Then in early 2003, a local friend introduced me to her sister whose books were carried in the bookstore chain that I'd been trying to get into for years. Her sister, who lived on the West coast, read my books and kindly gave them to her distributor with a personal recommendation. After several months of review, they agreed to distribute them and within a few months, the bookstore chain that I'd been pursuing for a decade purchased a batch of *Lord, Are You Sure?* to carry in their bookstores! Since that time, the same bookstore and many others have carried my various books.

When the time was right, it all flowed so effortlessly and the desires of my heart were granted. I never cease to marvel at how the Lord can use seemingly small and simple things to bring great things to pass. He knows the roads that will bring us to our desired destination. I didn't know that the bookstore chain I pursued only worked through specific distributors. I thought I could just keep sending books. But the Lord knew how the system worked.

I also believe that the Lord knew I wasn't ready ten years earlier. My talent needed polishing, and I needed experiences to teach me a message worth delivering. Had the Lord made this introduction three, five or ten years earlier, I wouldn't have had the skill or the message. But when the skills and the message were available, the doors opened easily.

Psalm 37:23 tells us that "The steps of a good man are ordered by the Lord; and He delighteth in his way. Though he fall, he shall not be utterly cast down; for the Lord upholdeth him with His hand."

It takes time to order our steps. Skills must be polished, knowledge attained, experience accumulated and relationship developed. While God can do all these instantaneously Himself – because He has all knowledge, we as human beings do not. Were He to pour the knowledge suddenly into our minds, it would not be the same as if we had worked, studied and attained it through experience.

Too many people give up when they initially meet failure. They put their desire on a shelf and assume that it is not meant to be. They don't realize that if you have the desire, then you have the power. An interesting byproduct of the relationships with my author friend and distributor is that they encouraged me to try my hand at fiction. As a young person in high school, I wanted to write fiction, but never thought I had what it took. I didn't think I could write the details. In the end, not only did I learn that I could do it, but I thoroughly enjoyed it! Writing fiction has become a wonderful blessing in my life – a treasure I never expected to find – an example of how the Lord doubles our talents when we use them.

If there is only one thing you learn from this story, let it be that if you have the desire, then you have the power - the greater the desire, the greater the power. Don't bury your righteous desires. Seek the Lord's guidance and direction as you study, learn and grow. Give Him time to order your steps as you hold onto your vision. Trust Him with the how and the when!

"Delight thyself in the Lord; and he shall give thee the desires of thine heart. Commit thy way unto the Lord; trust also in him; and he shall bring it to pass... Those who wait upon the Lord, they shall inherit the earth."(Psalms 37:4-5, 9)

Another example of the way the Lord takes care of things when we release the "How" to His care is when I developed a clear mental image of some changes we wanted around our house and property. I wrote a detailed description of how I wanted our property to look with a fenced in area for horses, a barn, and places for chickens and goats.

In keeping with these principles, I quit focusing on "how" or "how much" all of this would cost, but I did spend hours envisioning it. I never told anyone else of my dream – not even my husband. Nothing really happened toward it that I could see for about a month. Then one day in October of 2004, my nephew (who lives next door) called me and said he has a friend who raises horses and needed somewhere to graze them. In order to let them graze their horses in our field, my nephew wanted to put up a fence *exactly* where I've been envisioning it. I was floored, because the way he described the fence was exactly as I pictured it.

I asked him if that much fence would be expensive, but he said that his friend had the posts and that they would build it. I wholeheartedly agreed to his plan and told him about my vision for a barn, goats and horses and offered our help in building the fence. He loved the idea and so it began there.

I went for a walk on a Saturday afternoon a few weeks later and noticed that the gateposts along with several fence posts were in place. I took a walk to see where I'd like the barn to go and then sat down on a hay wagon facing the field. While I pictured it all in my mind, a car drove up and three people stepped out and started working on the fence. They were my nephew's friends who raise horses. I watched them drive several posts and reflected in wonder at the fact that all I had to do was envision it, and here it was being built right in front of my eyes - at absolutely no cost to me! Within another week, there were horses in our field!

I learned an important lesson from this. Sometimes we get too hung up on "how" we're going to make our dreams happen when really all we need to do is figure out "what" we want, ask the Lord for it, follow His promptings, and watch it unfold. Sometimes earning the money isn't even required. Normally, I would have tried to figure out how much money a fence would cost, set up a plan to save for it and rounded up enough people to build it. But this time, no effort on my part was even required. Each situation is different of course. Sometimes we must get out there and do the work. I'm certainly not advocating laziness. But sometimes, the Lord is willing to fight our battles for us, and all we need do is "stand still and see the salvation of the Lord" (Exodus 14:13)!

Points to Ponder

·   What would you dare to dream or pray for if "how it would happen" was no longer an issue?
·   List some times when you didn't know how it would all work out, but you put forth the necessary sacrifice, courage and faith to proceed anyway? How did it develop for your good?
·   Search the scriptures for individuals who didn't know how they'd obey the Lord's commands, but faithfully moved forward anyway.

Chapter 5: Where?

In Chapter 3 I shared the story of how we acquired our land on which to build. My family decided on a clear set of criteria for our property, and we began looking in Tennessee for it. We hadn't even considered Georgia. It wasn't that we felt anything extremely adverse to the state; we'd just always lived in Tennessee and loved it there. In the end, the Lord led us to a piece of property right across the border into Georgia that met our needs.

Ultimately, the move did more than give us the property we desired, it also put us in a position to make friends and associations that would greatly influence our lives and our children's lives in phenomenal ways. The Lord wanted us here for a reason – to serve and to be served.

Scripture is replete with examples of God making wonderful things happen in places one would never expect. Think about Joseph who was sold into Egypt. Who would think that the Lord could use him in prison? Yet, he did. Who would think an Israelite would be second in command only to Pharaoh over all of Egypt and help preserve that nation and Abraham's chosen family? Joseph's brothers certainly didn't!

Think of Moses who found his refuge in the house
of Pharoah's daughter. Surely, Moses' mother never
expected her son to find safety in the arms of the very
family who set out to kill him! Certainly Israel never
expected their deliverer to spring from the house of
their enemy - Pharoah's own courts! Moses never
expected to find God in the wilderness. Most of the
Israelites never believed they could find healing by
looking at a brass serpent on a pole, but those who
had the faith to look lived while those who refused
perished.

Ten of the twelve spies sent into Canaan didn't
have faith to believe that God could give them a
Promised Land inhabited by giants. The lad Samuel
didn't expect to hear God's voice in the middle of the
night. He came to Eli three times before he finally
understood that God spoke to him and would call
him as the next prophet in Israel.

When Samuel came to the house of Jesse in search
of the next King of Israel, he expected to select one of
Jesse's older strapping sons. But the Lord told
Samuel, "Look not on his countenance, or on the
height of his stature; because I have refused him: for
the Lord seeth not as man seeth; for man looketh on
the outward appearance, but the Lord looketh on the
heart." Samuel asked if there were not another son,

and Jesse told him of his youngest son David who tended the flocks. That day, God selected a mere lad, the youngest of Jesse's family as the next king of Israel. The Philistines never expected their hero Goliath to be slain by this same scrawny little Israelite youth.

Who would expect the King of Kings and Lord of Lords to be born in the obscure village of Bethlehem in a lowly stable? When Philip told Nathaneal, "We have found him of whom Moses in the law and the prophets did write, Jesus of Nazareth, the son of Joseph," Nathaneal replied doubtfully, "Can there any good thing come out of Nazareth?"

Time and again the Lord has shown us that things are not always as they appear. Miracles rarely come from where we expect. "God hath chosen the foolish things of the world to confound the wise; and God hath chosen the weak things of the world to confound the things which are mighty" (1 Corinthians 1: 27).

When we relinquish our need to control and our expectations about from where our deliverance will come, we open ourselves up to a whole new world of possibilities.

A good example of getting a clear picture of what you want, but not limiting the Lord to where it comes from is something that happened to my second oldest sister. Lisa was about twenty six and unmarried, but she wanted very much to have a family of her own with a good faithful man. She had a clear idea of the type of man she wanted to marry. She wanted a man who belonged to her same denomination with similar beliefs and values as her own. Yet locally, she could not find anyone among those she dated who felt like the right match for her. She had several marriage proposals, but none felt right.

One weekend she and a friend drove all the way from Tennessee to Ohio to a single adult Church conference. During that weekend, she met a man who fit her criteria. But he lived in Chicago, and she lived in Tennessee! They didn't let this stand in their way, though. By the end of the conference, they both knew that they had met their future spouse. I remember my sister coming home from this weekend and telling me she'd met the man she would marry.

She did, and he's been a wonderful husband. They lived in Chicago for several years and then moved down to Tennessee where they built a home and are raising their two fine sons to love and serve the Lord.

If my sister had been too scared to travel outside her comfort zone, she never would have met her husband. She didn't limit the location from which God could deliver her miracle, and in the end she's been richly blessed.

Points to Ponder

· Search your memory for times when your blessings or answers came from a place you never expected. Document these in your journal

· Search the scriptures and ponder upon those instances were deliverance came from an unusual place or source. For example, what lesson did Jonah learn about not misjudging a "place" or an entire city of people?

· How will you keep your options open in the future and look for deliverance and miracles to originate anywhere - perhaps even from your trials?

Chapter 6: What?

Thus far, we've talked a lot about the things we can't control. But there is one very important thing we can, and that is "What" we want. Jesus repeatedly told us to ask, knock, and seek.

Yet, of all the questions, I think it's ironic that most of us never get clear on "What" we want. Oh, we do in a few areas. We might want a bigger home, a better life, a spouse, etc. But few of us get specific about exactly what we want. We don't take the time to clearly envision the house or how we want our life to feel and look or what characteristics we want in a spouse.

Most of the time we just whine or complain about what we don't have, but we don't get a vivid picture of what we want it to be like. For example, I often griped about my old clunker van, but I didn't decide what I wanted instead. I was too afraid to ask for what I really wanted, too afraid of what it might cost or what debt might be incurred to obtain it. Not until I got very clear on the make, model, year, style and features did what we want become available to us.

Get Specific

Where most of us fail is that we never really ask. We just whine. We don't get precise in describing what we want. If you don't ask specifically, you can't receive specifically.

A little incident happened to me in February of 2005 that taught me a lesson in asking with precision. My nephew composes songs, plays the guitar and sings. He's quite the talented young man, and we always enjoy listening to him at family gatherings. There are a couple old songs that he plays that I really enjoy. One is an old haunting melody called *Long Black Veil* and the other is *Folsom Prison.*

Before my nephew left to serve a two-year mission in the Dominican Republic in February of 2005, I asked him to "record those songs you sing for me." He promised he would and true to his word, the day before he left, he locked himself in his room and recorded a tape for me. But when I received the tape that night, I found three newer songs that he'd written. I do enjoy them, but they aren't the songs I wanted. You see I didn't ask specifically. I didn't say, "Noah, please record *Long Black Veil* and *Folsom Prison* for me." I just said, "Noah, please record those songs you sing before you leave."

Like a loving nephew, he recorded songs he sings for me. He genuinely wanted to give me what I asked for, but I wasn't specific!

Sometimes in life we don't get specific about what we want, and we get something, but it may not be exactly what we wanted. We need to pinpoint what we want. How else will we recognize it when it arrives? The next time you set a goal, don't let it be a vague, misty concept but a clear, concise request! Then put it in writing. If you've put your objective in writing, and then your prayer is answered, neither you nor anyone else can deny that the Lord brought it to pass.

Write It Down

When I was about seventeen or eighteen years old, a teacher at church suggested we make a list of the characteristics we wanted in a spouse. I itemized 100 very specific characteristics I wanted in a husband and kept it in my journal. When I had been dating Greg Pehrson for about five months, my college roommates and I were sitting around looking at my list. One of my friends suggested I run Greg down the list. As a lark, I did, and he met 96 out of 100 items. I was quite startled because up until this time, I didn't seriously consider him as a marriage possibility.

Another roommate said, "Wow, have you prayed about this?"

"No! And I'm not going to!" I retorted adamantly. I didn't want to get married. I was a freshman in college with my heart set on a career.

Over the next few weeks the Lord made clear to me that I did need to pray about the matter. When I did, I received a clear, firm answer that Greg was the man I should marry. We were engaged within a week of my answer and married six months later. If I hadn't had a clear written picture of what I wanted in a husband, I don't know how long it would have taken, or even if I would have recognized him as the man God intended for me to marry.

Use Gratitude to Shift Your Attitude

Jesus taught, "Ask, and it shall be given you; seek, and ye shall find; knock, and it shall be opened unto you: For every one that asketh receiveth; and he that seeketh findeth; and to him that knocketh it shall be opened. Or what man is there of you, whom if his son ask bread, will he give him a stone? Or if he ask a fish, will he give him a serpent?" (Matthew 7:7-10)

Paul taught in Philippians 4:6 "Don't be unduly concerned about anything; but in every thing by prayer and supplication with thanksgiving let your requests be made known unto God."

Notice Paul told us to ASK with Thanksgiving and to let our requests be made known with THANKSGIVING. Think about that! How do you ask someone for something and thank them for it at the same time? The only way to do that is if you sincerely expect the person to answer. You have faith in them and their desire to help you.

God wants to give good things to his children, but nowhere does He say, "gripe and ye shall receive" or "whine and complain and it shall be opened unto you." He simply said to ask. Asking requires clarity about what you want. Once we've asked and we've received an answer or a feeling of peace, we should expect that what we've asked for will arrive in God's good time.

James 1:5-6 tells us to "ask in faith, nothing wavering." But sometimes we become discouraged, and we fall back into griping or doubting. It can be difficult to hold the right attitude – an attitude of faith and expectant hope - when circumstances appear as if you're standing still or moving in reverse.

Are you like me? Whenever I hit a problem or challenge, my initial human reaction is one of the following:

- get angry, upset or pout
- start to lose faith that things are going to work out
- blame myself or others for my misfortune
- give up hope
- assume God is giving me a "serpent" when I asked for a "fish."

None of these are productive or healthy. Each of these reactions slackens my hope, weakens my faith, and distances me from God and my worthwhile goals. For you see, all the promises are unto them who *believe*. None of these human reactions foster faith – none of them persuades one to *believe*. Without faith, nothing happens.

Draw Upon the Clarity and Power of Gratitude

Since 2004, I've performed a series of "experiments" (for lack of a better word) on the

principle of gratitude. These tests have been
extremely enlightening and quite effective in not only
shifting my attitude from doubt to faith but also in
unlocking blessings from the Lord. I think the reason
for this has been two fold. First it has forced me to get
specific about what I want. I have to state what I
want in a detailed, positive way. Second, it helps me
hold faith and expectant gratitude. Third, I have
written proof that I asked and also a reminder of
what my goal is.

STEP 1: Decide "what" you want and "when" you want it.

Since experimenting with the principle of
gratitude, I've tried to turn myself around when I
catch myself reacting to a disappointment in a
negative way. Instead of entertaining myself with a
pity party, I force myself to examine the situation and
ask: what would have to happen in this situation to
make me feel better about it? What do I want?

For example, when my refrigerator and car broke
down in the same week, I asked myself what would
resolve the situation to my satisfaction. I wanted
them both fixed, and I wanted it done in a specific
time and within a certain budget.

When the car I'd purchased with my savings only three months prior blew a gasket, I asked myself what solution would satisfy me. What I really wanted was to stop driving 10-year-old vehicles! I spent more on repairs and replacing them than I would with a car payment on a newer vehicle. I wanted a van still under warranty that ran well and that I could rely on to take our six children where they needed to go. Instead of settling for what I could "get by on," I decided what would make me feel satisfied and secure in our mode of transportation.

STEP 2: Pray and get a confirmation that your desires are in harmony with God's will for you.

The next step is to pray about your desires and ask for a confirmation that what you want is what God wants for you. For example, in the case of the desire for a new van, I prayed for a couple weeks about whether it was what God wanted for our family before the answer finally came – literally within a few hours before the decision had to be made.

STEP 3: Write a gratitude statement and repeat it.

I am about to explain how I use a gratitude statement to shift my thinking. Please note that there is nothing magical or mystical about a gratitude statement other than that it shifts your own mind from fear to faith and from doubt to belief. Remember that faith is the "substance of things hoped for and the evidence of things not seen" (Hebrews 11:1).Your ability to muster faith is critical in your ability to take possession of blessings. Thus, a gratitude statement is simply a tool to help you achieve a level of faith that God can use to bring about your "miracle."

A gratitude statement should be written in the present tense and start with something like, "I am so happy and grateful now that..." It should end with a statement that ensures that everything happens in the best way. For example, I use, "I am so excited, thrilled and amazed to see these things happening in ways that are for the highest good for us and all concerned. Thank you!"

Here's an example of a gratitude statement at work. One time, because of some unexpected expenditures, I didn't have the money to meet some important obligations. My initial reaction was to get upset and begin to doubt. But then I remembered that on so many occasions the Lord has pulled us through in a pinch. He has confirmed to me time and again that He will care for us if we will put our trust in Him. So, pulling myself up by the bootstraps, I took a break from my pity party and decided to use gratitude to change my attitude.

Instead of giving up hope and assuming the worst, I forced myself to take a hard look at my finances and make a list of what was due by a specific date. I totaled it up and decided on the dollar value that would satisfy my obligations and would meet our family's needs for a given period of time. In this case it was a 3-day period. I decided on the dollar amount needed within this time frame to meet our obligations.

It was a rather large amount and while my husband and I each had paychecks coming in over the next three days, they would only cover two-thirds of the amount needed. The rest would have to come from somewhere else. Instead of worrying about "how" this would happen, I crafted a gratitude statement which I began to repeat to myself. It went something like this:

"I am so happy and grateful now that at least $X in funds are flowing into my bank accounts by [Specific Date] enabling us to meet all our needs and

obligations for this period of time. I am excited,
thrilled and amazed to see this happening in ways
that are for the highest good for us and all concerned.
Thank you!"

After offering a prayer of thanks that what I
needed was on its way, I began repeating the
statement in my mind and aloud. Remember it's not
God I was trying to convince – it was myself! The first
day – when I felt most discouraged – I repeated it
nearly a hundred times. I'd say it out loud as I drove
down the road or in my mind as I cleaned my house.
Amazingly enough, my negative attitude quickly
shifted to one of hope and positive expectation. I
began to get excited to see how the Lord would make
that money flow into my bank accounts. The
following days I started my day by repeating the
gratitude statement several times or whenever a
discouraging doubt crept into my mind.

At the end of the deadline, we were still about
10% short of the amount specified, but things had
happened over those days to allow me more time to
meet certain obligations. In the end, we had what we
needed when we needed it. The Lord provided.

I have used gratitude to activate blessings time
and again. While my deadlines are not always met,
my needs are. In the activation of blessings, you

specify the "what" and "why" and let God take care of the rest. It's an exercise in faith and patience, but it is amazing how gratitude can turn around your attitude and give you faith when you don't think you can muster another ounce of it.

The Gratitude Journal Entry

Another way to write a gratitude statement is to paint a vivid picture by writing a future journal entry. Either on a piece of paper or in your journal, create a journal entry for a future date by which you will achieve your objective. Put the future date at the top and then write your gratitude statement something like this:

[Future date]

I am so happy and grateful now that…. Because now…. [Paint a complete description of what it will look like, feel like and be like to have the desires of your heart. Explain why it's a good thing now that you have it or that things worked out as they did. State this all in positive terms. Each phrase should stand alone as a positive statement. For example, replace phrases like "I'm not sick anymore" with "I am healthy and feel energetic, etc." Or replace "I don't have any debts" with "all my financial obligations are met in full and I am financially

free."] Then conclude with something like ... I am excited,
thrilled and amazed to see this all happen in ways that
are for the highest good for me and all concerned. Thank
you!

Write this journal entry in the present tense as if
it's already yours and has already happened. If it
doesn't happen by the specified date, don't give up.
We're not always the best predictors of how long
something's going to take. Adjust the date, and keep
working toward it with an eye of faith.

Special Note

Many people have trouble writing or repeating a
statement phrased like: "I am so happy and grateful
now that...." when they don't feel like they have it
yet. For those who struggle with believing in
something they cannot see, I would remind you of 1
John 5:14-15: "This is the confidence that we have in
him, that, if we ask any thing **according to his will**,
he hears us: And if we know that he hears us,
whatsoever we ask, we know that **we have** the
petitions that we desired of him."

Remember, He says you *have them*! Especially if
you've followed these steps and obtained a
confirmation that what you ask is in harmony with

God's will, then you have the petitions of your heart! They're yours! They've left the building and are on their way to you. It's just a matter of time to receive the delivery.

To recap, here are the steps for using gratitude to shift your attitude so God can adjust your altitude:

1. Decide "what" you want and "when" you want it. Although "when" isn't something you can control, it never hurts to ask as part of your specifics!

2. Pray and get a confirmation that your desires are in harmony with God's will for you.

3. Remember that once you have your confirmation, you have it! It's yours. It's just a matter of holding your faith and gratitude and patiently waiting for its delivery.

4. Write a gratitude statement and repeat it as much as you can. The objective here is to bolster your faith and your belief.

5. Act immediately upon any promptings you receive from the Lord on what to do or how to proceed.

6. Continue to express gratitude to God even if things do not develop exactly when or how you specified.

As we cultivate a continual spirit of gratitude, we draw nearer to God from whom all blessings flow. Try the power of gratitude the next time life throws you a lemon and see if God won't help you turn it into sweet lemonade.

Don't Settle for Less Than You Need

In the spring of 2004, our 20 year old van had seen better days and we decided I needed a newer car to drive. Since what I really wanted was a 2003 Chrysler Town & Country mini-van, and since we didn't have the cash for that nor did we wish to go into debt for it, I decided to buy a large used car. We shopped around and settled upon a 1992 Lincoln Town Car. For three months, it drove fine and while the kids and I were a bit squished, it drove smoothly and was immensely safer than my pitiful old van.

Then, after owning the car for only three months, it blew a gasket and would cost almost as much as I paid for the car to fix it. I'd spent my savings paying cash for the lemon, and now we were back to driving the old van. After a few times driving it, I realized just how unsafe it was. Greg and I began praying about getting a new car. This time I decided to ask the Lord for what we really wanted. I prayed about it and felt okay, but still didn't feel as if I had a clear answer. My husband prayed and felt good about getting the new van and felt the Lord would provide a way.

But I still wasn't sure, and I wanted to be absolutely certain! I didn't want to lean on my husband's answer alone. I knew obtaining the van would require a car payment, and if I didn't know 100% beyond any doubt that this decision was correct, then I'd constantly worry over the payments and whether we did the right thing. So I fasted and prayed. A couple weeks went by with still no definite answer. Meanwhile, we shopped around and found a good deal on a 2003 Chrysler Town & Country minivan.

We planned to drive to Marietta, Georgia to look at the van and buy it on a specific day. We had to rent a car just to drive down there because the vehicles we owned wouldn't make the trip. I went to pick up the rental car right before we were to leave for Marietta and on the way home, I finally got my answer. It came so vividly and clearly that I could not deny it.

The following event in the New Testament entered my mind. When Jesus and his disciples came into Capernaum, the people who received tribute money came to Peter and asked him if his Master paid tribute. Peter affirmed that he did. As they started to go into the house, Jesus stopped Peter and told him, "lest we should offend them, go thou to the sea, and cast an hook, and take up the fish that first cometh up; and when thou hast opened his mouth, thou shalt find a piece of money: that take, and give unto them for me and thee" (Matthew 17:24-27).

The Lord's assurance came: "Stop worrying about money. If I can get money from a fish, I can get you what you need when you need it. I need you and your family in my service." The Lord had a work for us to do that involved having reliable transportation. I not only knew the choice to be right, but also why it was right, and what blessings the Lord would give us if we used the van in His service! We bought the van and the Lord has more than provided.

There are things the Lord needs us to do. He needs tongues to share his truth and hands to do His work. Sometimes objects are required for you to be able to serve Him. And when that is the case, He most definitely will provide. In this instance, I also felt an overwhelming love from my Father in Heaven that He truly did want to give good things to us!

God can easily manipulate things to bring you the resources you need. Just as he could tell Peter exactly where to go, where to cast his hook, and which fish to look inside, He can tell us where to go and what to do to find the things we need.

I learned that the Lord looks at a broader canvas than I do. I was like a person studying a mural with her nose stuck to the wall. I focused on the here and now, assuming that indebting ourselves for reliable transportation was a step backwards. But in those few moments, the Lord taught me that He has something bigger for our family than what we could see from our myopic viewpoint. For a few moments, the Lord pulled my nose away from the canvas long enough to catch a glimpse of the big picture and how this one particular decision fit into His plan.

With that glimpse, everything made sense, and knowing His plan made the required leap of faith much simpler. It gave our family our "marching orders" for the next season of our lives and I just love it when the Lord gives "marching orders!" It's wonderful to know what He wants to happen and how what you're doing fits into that plan. It fills you with joy and gives you faith to believe in the best and to keep persevering in spite of difficulties.

The Big Vision

Some people have difficulty deciding what they want. They're too afraid that they'll choose the wrong thing or that by making one choice they eliminate other choices. In the end, they choose inaction and their progression stalls. I've been like that to some degree. While I generally have no problem setting short term goals for things I want, I've had difficulty selecting a big vision – the dream I choose to work toward.

Using gratitude to set short term goals and work toward them has a wonderful benefit in helping you actively build your faith muscles. Instead of waiting for life to bring you trials and force you to grow, you take control of the day-to-day elements of your life and consciously choose where you want to go and let faith in God carry you to your desired destination.

While doing this, one should still have a big picture of how they want their life to look, feel and be. Without a clear destination, we tend to be like a mouse turning a wheel one more round, but going nowhere. That was my problem. I had been using these principles for two years before I finally realized that I had neglected to solidify the big picture for my life.

Greg and I had been struggling under a load of debt, and all I could focus on was getting rid of it. My mentor in the principles of abundant living, Leslie Householder, repeatedly advised me not to focus on the debt. She said I needed to focus on something positive. Focusing on the debt would only cause it to remain. Whatever we give our focus, feeling and energy to grows. It's a law of nature. Debt was the last place I should have been putting my focus and feeling!

In an effort to keep the word "debt" out of my goals, I began working toward short term goals – monthly amounts of money we should earn that would meet our obligations and whittle them down over time. I did this for nearly two years with very little, if any, significant progress in the reduction of our debts.

Then one Friday in September of 2004, Leslie and I spoke on the phone about how things were going for us, and she asked me what I really want from life. I admitted to her that while we were doing well, we weren't making a significant dent in our debts – which is really what I wanted to happen. She challenged me to dream big. Again, she reiterated that I needed to stop focusing on the debt and challenged me to picture my life after it was gone. Up

YOU CAN'T FLY IF YOU'RE STILL CLUTCHING THE DIRT   111

until this time, I just couldn't think past the debt or picture what my life would be like without it.

One thing she suggested was that Greg and I pretend to shop at the mall, use fake checks and write them out and see if we could spend $50,000. Of course, we weren't to give the store owners the checks! It would be an exercise in dreaming and in expanding our minds to the possibilities. I told her it was depressing to window shop because we didn't have the money for things. She told me that it's good to get depressed sometimes because it makes you aggravated and mad enough to change and do something about your situation.

Later that day I spoke with my longtime friend, Alanna Webb, telling her what Leslie said. She suggested that perhaps I got my thrill in life from pulling myself out of a tight financial spot. I had grown accustomed to making up the difference... leaning on the Lord and using gratitude to help me out of a pinch. She suggested that it had become a thrill for me. To a degree it was! In essence, I had become addicted to leaning on the Lord to pull us out of a tight spot and then getting excited when once more He did it. She suggested that if I could find my thrill elsewhere, then I might be able to break the cycle.

At this point I realized that evidently something was wrong in my thinking. I knew the principles of abundant living. I practiced gratitude, I could draw on the powers of heaven, and the Lord would pull us through, but something still wasn't right. I began praying, "Please teach me how to think!" That prayer led to one of my greatest breakthroughs... not only did I need to get clear on "what" I wanted but "why" I wanted it!

"Commit thy works unto the LORD, and thy thoughts shall be established." Proverbs 16: 3

Points to Ponder

· What do you want from life? What would your ideal life look like, feel like, be like? What would bring you the most joy and happiness?
· Have you taken the time to prayerfully seek a confirmation from the Lord that the things you want are the ones He wants for you?
· Are you grateful now for the things you have and for the things that are on their way to you?

Chapter 7: Why?

In the fall of 2004, we decided we should probably refinance our house and consolidate debts, but I didn't have much faith that it would appraise for what we needed because our six children had done quite a bit of damage to the house over the years. For example, they'd busted a doorframe, colored and knocked holes in the walls, and broken a pedestal sink in my office bathroom. After the pedestal sink being broken for a year, I finally replaced it a couple weeks before my conversations with Leslie and Alanna. It felt great to finally have it fixed.

The Saturday after realizing that I'd been focusing on short-term fixes, I had a dream. I dreamed that our second oldest son Joshua held up our younger son Nate so he could stand on the pedestal sink, and they broke it. I woke up angry – a realization striking me that my entire life was like that – I fix it, they break it, I pay the debt and the interest or a crisis keeps bringing it back. I was going nowhere! A picture of a mouse on a treadmill came to mind – I constantly repaired, repaid and fixed something that re-broke or never went away. It depressed me so incredibly to finally realize that all the "progress" I thought I'd been making for the previous two years wasn't really progress. I wasn't going anywhere – wasn't making any headway in eliminating debt or getting anywhere.

I was a rat on a wheel!

That same morning I had a full blown argument with one of our children that left me in tears and feeling like a horrible mother. I went off by myself and had a breakdown. Everything felt hopeless. To know that I had all the tools, yet still managed to go nowhere was more than I could take. I ended up crying so hard that my eyes were bloodshot and swollen. It all felt so hopeless. Here I thought I'd been learning things and using the laws and the principles Leslie had taught me, but in reality they just helped me turn the wheel one more rotation.

That was the start of the most depressing week of my life. Later that afternoon I went to a leadership meeting for church and the instructor giving the lesson played a CD with a stirring rendition of the hymn, "Be Still My Soul." I love that version of the song and something she said – which I can't even remember now - made me get the message.

"If you want to get off the treadmill – BE STILL!"

Of course, it made absolute perfect sense! In order
to stop spinning, I had to stop and step off the wheel.
But, how could I be still? I had to work and earn
money and support our family and make up the
difference. How could I just be still and do nothing?

Yet, I felt depressed enough to try anything! I took
an entire week and didn't work other than what was
necessary to maintain my Web sites. I spent all my
time cleaning the house – it needed it badly and it
was the only thing that felt right. I dove into house
work and thought about what I wanted out of life.
Alanna helped me work through an important issue.
I realized I already had everything I wanted – I just
didn't want to owe anyone for it, and there were a
few home improvements and additions we'd like to
make to make our home more orderly, attractive and
unifying. She suggested I visualize a mortgage
burning party with all my friends there and the
mortgage paid in full on our house where we owned
it outright and it looked the way I wanted it. Now
this I could get excited about! I had my "why!"

I started picturing a big brass platter with Greg
holding our mortgage papers over it and me lighting
a match beneath. All our friends and family gathered
around and celebrated with us. The house looked just
how I want it with the garage and family room over

it, the sunroom, deck and pool, new furnishings, hardwood floors, a fenced in area for horses, a red barn and the landscape well-kept. I now had a vision that would motivate and propel me forward! Leslie suggested I write it down in detail, then distill it into a paragraph I could put on a note card with a date at the top like a journal entry. I did that and soon it became a vision that I called to mind anytime I became discouraged.

The more I envisioned, the more I realized I had something I could get excited about! I could sink my teeth into a feeling of relaxed freedom! I could get motivated about opening up our home to friends and family and sharing the blessings God has given us with others. I could get excited about developing our farm so that our children learned responsibility and how to appreciate the gifts of nature. I now had a whole list of "why's" that would inspire and motivate me.

During my week or so of 'being still' all I felt compelled to do was work on the house. It felt like the right time to refinance. My oldest son and I painted, weeded the yard, patched holes, and painted. We hired someone to pressure wash the outside of the house. We did everything we could before the appraiser came. Yet, still there were things undone – things that it was just humanly impossible for me to tackle on my own. I said a prayer and put it into Heavenly Father's hands. If it was meant to be, it would be. In the end, it appraised for more than we needed. We consolidated the bulk of our debts into a payment less than our original house payment!

This left us with a car payment and a debt I owed a family member. I really wanted that family member paid back. It's been a burden on my mind for several years.

A few months later we decided to get an equity line on our house and pay everything else off. We had the application turned in and right in the middle of the approval process, my husband lost his job. There was a very real possibility the loan would be denied with him not having a job. This time I just let go of it. I didn't worry. I told the Lord if it was meant to be, it would be and it was in His hands. We ended up getting the loan. With that loan and my husband's severance, the mountain of debt moved in a matter of a few months from the time I finally started looking at the big picture instead of focusing on short term fixes.

You wouldn't think a vision of a mortgage burning party would lead to consolidating all your debts into a mortgage, but until this happened, we could never make any significant progress paying twenty-something percent interest. A single digit interest rate on our home loan would make all the difference. Now all the money we've been applying toward debts is actually attacking the principle instead of simply covering the ever accruing interest!

Interestingly enough, even with my husband's job loss we didn't worry. We knew it was for a reason. I've spent the last 15 years getting to do what I love while my husband's been stuck in a job he hated. The Lord took those years to help me build a business that could sustain us. He moved our mountain of debt just in time to coincide with Greg's chance to follow his dream. Now my husband can enjoy his work and focus on doing what he wants to do – building his own personal chef business. Plus, him being at home more is having a wonderful affect on our family life and helping to create a secure, consistent, and more harmonious atmosphere. God's timing is always perfect and His ways are always the best!

It's All About Emotions

Over time, I refined my goal and looked past the event of a mortgage burning party to a general view of our lives, our home and the feelings we would experience when things were orderly, peaceful, secure, harmonious, abundant and unified. In time I learned a very important lesson. *We think we want "things" but in reality it's just a feeling we're after. When we discover that we can feel that feeling anytime we choose, that feeling puts us in harmony with the people, things, circumstances and events that enhance, amplify and draw toward us more of the same desired emotions.*

It wasn't things that I wanted – wasn't necessarily the barn or the fence, horses, hardwood floors or a pool. Those things would be nice, but it was more that they painted a picture in my mind of the feeling I wanted to create in my life. What is important for me is to know that I'm making a difference for good in the world. My heart's desire is a home and family life that conveys feelings of peace, security, abundance, plenty, order, harmony, gratitude, love, unity, cooperation, and joy in which the Spirit of the Lord can readily dwell.

Once I realized that the feelings were what I wanted, and not necessarily "things" or "money" or even my "debts paid off," I discovered that I could feel those feelings at any time. I already had the ability to feel them either in my mind or even in my existing world. They were already there if I chose to see them and foster them. But I had to get off that rat wheel and "be still" to do that.

As a husband and wife, we began working toward this atmosphere in our home. We began striving as a family to keep our home orderly, peaceful and harmonious. As we fostered these feelings, more good things came our way. Of course we struggled; of course things aren't perfect all of the time. Sometimes there are messes. Sometimes there are arguments. But we're working toward those feelings we've identified as the desires of our heart. As we do this, each piece to the picture starts falling into place. It has to, because we are now living in harmony with the things, people, circumstances and events that will amplify and enhance those positive and uplifting feelings.

What Is Your Why?

In the formula which says that your focus, faith and feeling bring miracles to pass, your feeling is your "why." Without a clear and compelling "why" for accomplishing what you want, you won't make significant progress.

You have to experience some strong emotion. For some, that's excitement over a goal. For others it's getting mad enough or disgusted enough with the way things are to do something about it. In my case, I had to get depressed enough to change the way I thought. I had to get upset enough to step off my treadmill and take a good hard look at my life. I had to get a clear picture of my goal and why I wanted it.

What is your why? What feelings do you want to experience in your life and why do you want them? You can control your why. It's very important that your why is one that resonates with your spirit and feels right. It is only between you and God, but bring Him into the discussion about your "why." For example, if I choose to be a best selling author because I want to be mega rich and have everyone fall all over me with praise and accolades, then I think God would consider that a waste of time and may decide it's not such an admirable goal for me. Then again, He could very well give it to me and teach me that it's not all it's cracked up to be.

But if I choose to be a best selling author so I can promote good in the world in an impactful way, because I want to teach truth and make a positive impact on a generation or even future generations by writing a classic, then perhaps He'd see that as something He could support. The accolades might even be there... but they aren't my objective.

A Caution on "Why"

While we can control "Why" we want what we want, we should avoid asking useless "Why" questions. For example, very little can come of the pity party questions: "Why me? Why now? Why us?" These are all useless questions. When you're prone to shake your fist at the heavens and ask why something has happened to you, replace that "Why" with a "What" question. For example, these types of questions will help you find answers:

- What can I learn from this?
- What will I do now that I wouldn't have done otherwise?
- What can I do for others because of this situation?
- What do I want to have happen?
- What would need to happen for me to feel comfortable with this situation?

Use these questions to help you decide what you want to have happen next so that you can intelligently and specifically approach the Lord and ask for a solution. Whining and crying "Why me? Why now? Why us?" will get you nowhere. Be proactive and decide what solution you want and then gratefully ask for it!

Points to Ponder

- Why do you want the things you want? What is the big, compelling reason that makes you work toward and patiently seek your dream(s)?
- Are you focusing on the big picture or are you getting lost in the details? Are you spinning your wheels or being still and trusting God?
- Have you gotten too caught up in wanting "things" rather than getting to the root feelings that bring you joy and happiness? How can you evaluate and if necessary change this?
- How can you open your mind to the possibility that your Heavenly Father could bring you the feelings and desires of your heart in a different way than the method or vehicle you expect? In other words, is it possible that He could fulfill the needs and desires of your heart through alternate means than you think? Are you open to this possibility?
- How can you release the useless "why" questions that only lead to whining and ingratitude?

Chapter 8: Relax Your Grip & Fly!

Jesus taught, "Give, and it shall be given unto you; good measure, pressed down, and shaken together, and running over, shall men give into your bosom. For with the same measure that ye mete withal it shall be measured to you again" (Luke 6: 38).

The imagery of a relaxed, open palm comes to my mind when I think of giving and also when I think about the principles we've discussed thus far. It's that same relaxed open palm my father had with the bird when it ceased to struggle. It's the opposite of the term "tight fisted" which is often used to describe someone who is greedy and selfish.

One of my favorite depictions of the Savior is the Christus by Danish sculptor Bertel Thorvaldsen. It's a snow white marble statue of the Savior with his arms outstretched, palms open, the tokens of the remarkable sacrifice He made for me engraven upon the palms of His hands (Isaiah 49:15-16). As I stand before this statue, it is as if He beckons me, "Come unto me, all ye that labor and are heavy laden, and I will give you rest. Take my yoke upon you, and learn of me; for I am meek and lowly in heart: and ye shall find rest unto your souls" (Matthew 11:28-30).

Besides the matchless gift those scars represent, His open palms symbolize all that He stands for, died for, everything He is, and everything He teaches and exemplifies. His hands are the opposite of the clenched fists so commonly found in this hardened world. His outstretched palms are the antithesis of tight-fisted greed, unforgiving, self-centeredness or stinginess.

With Him there is an overflowing abundance of love, kindness, mercy, longsuffering, forgiveness, patience and a desire to do good, lift, build and bless. Was there even once that He turned someone away for being too old, too young, too rich, too poor? Did He ever command, "Go away, there's not enough for you here?" Did He ever say, "Oh, you're too far gone, there's nothing I can do for you now?" Never!

If we could only live as the Savior lives and love as He loves! I believe happiness and peace only come to us in this troubled world when we strive to live as He lives, as we release our need for control, our desire to dominate, to be right, to get the last word, and our compulsion to tenaciously hang onto the things we possess.

He taught, "But love ye your enemies, and do good, and lend, hoping for nothing again; and your reward shall be great, and ye shall be the children of the Highest: for he is kind unto the unthankful and to the evil."

"Be ye therefore merciful, as your Father also is merciful. Judge not, and ye shall not be judged: condemn not, and ye shall not be condemned: forgive, and ye shall be forgiven: Give, and it shall be given unto you; good measure, pressed down, and shaken together, and running over, shall men give into your bosom. For with the same measure that ye mete withal it shall be measured to you again" (Luke 6:35-38).

How easily we forget that every good thing we have comes from Him! Every gift, talent, and resource emanates from Him. It is only when we come to trust in His abundance - His boundless ability to forgive, to love, to bless and supply all our needs - that we relinquish our tight-fisted hold on the things of the world and experience the blessings He has in store for us. He put it this way, "For whosoever will save his life shall lose it: and whosoever will lose his life for my sake shall find it." (Matthew 16:25).

A person who believes in scarcity hangs on to their time, their talents, their money and their resources. After all, they might not get more! A person who fully trusts the Lord and understands what they can control and what the Lord controls, completely relaxes her grip on the world around her because she knows there's plenty and to spare. She's also tuned into the Source from which all blessings flow. Thus, she's free to in Christ-like ways give, serve, lift and build others up.

In order to fly and reach our full potential as a child of God, we must relax our grip on the things of the earth! We have to trust that if we need food, raiment, money, shelter, time or other resources that they will be there for us when we need them. A clear indicator of someone who has reached this state of being is their possession of a generous, giving and serving personality.

When we think about all our Heavenly Father has done for us – all our Savior has done for us – we naturally want to give something to God in return, don't we? We want to grow closer to Him, to know his will, to know God's thoughts.

James 4: 8 says "Draw nigh to God, and He will draw nigh to you."

There are at least four things that you can give to the Lord – ways you can draw close to Him so that He will in turn draw nigh to you. When you do these things, He immediately blesses you, and thus you are forever in His debt. But it is a blessed debt!

First, Offer an Obedient and Humble Heart

Jesus said, "If ye love me, keep my commandments" (John 14:15). He also explained how we can tell whether a principle is true, "If any man will do his will, he shall know of the doctrine whether it be of God or whether I speak of myself" (John 7:17).

When we obey the commandments of God we are blessed. The Lord is bound when we do what He says. When we don't do what He says, we have no promise. Look at it this way: There are laws in place and these laws have consequences whenever you break them or whenever you keep them. If you break a law, you incur the negative consequences. If you obey a law, you reap the rewards associated with that law. When we receive any blessing from the Lord it is by obedience to that law upon which it is based.

The Lord hasn't given us commandments just as a suggestion. They aren't ways for Him to control us or have power over us. He gave them to us because He loves us and wants us to be happy. And He knows that happiness comes when we obey these laws. When we humble ourselves and realize that our Father in Heaven knows best about what's going to make us happy, we submit to His commandments. As a result, we gain a witness that they are from God by the blessings we receive for our obedience.

Second, Have a Servant's Heart

Jesus taught, "whosoever will be chief among you, let him be your servant: Even as the Son of man came not to be ministered unto, but to minister, and to give his life a ransom for many" (Matthew 20: 27).

Draw close to the Lord through selfless service. When you are in the service of your fellow beings, you are only in the service of your God. "Do unto others as you'd have them do unto you." Jesus taught us to go the extra mile, give to him that ask, love our neighbors and love our enemies, bless those that curse us, do good to those who hate us and pray for them who despitefully use us and persecute us (Matthew 5:41-44).

Look for ways to use your time and talents to serve others. There is no greater joy than in using the gifts the Lord has given you to bless those around you. That's why He gave them to you in the first place!

Third, Donate Generous Tithes and Offerings

Do you struggle with making ends meet? Do you wrestle with debt or need help with managing your money wisely? The Lord has a solution!

Most of the time when we read Malachi 3:8-11 we think of the law of tithing and how the Lord promises to open the windows of heaven for our sake when we are honest with Him and give Him ten percent of our increase. Tithing is a principle I've been taught and practiced since childhood. I've found that paying tithing has blessed me with the things I need when I needed them. We may scrape by financially but somehow the money we need appears when we need it most, or we'll be given the wisdom to get by on what we have. The windows of heaven have opened for me spiritually and physically in knowledge, wisdom and understanding.

But I'll be honest with you, I'm not the best money manager in the world and monetarily-speaking I don't know that you could say that the windows of heaven have poured me out more money than I could receive! Perhaps you know what it's like when it feels like every dollar you earn is already earmarked by the interest monster. Or maybe you know what it's like when no matter how much you make, you still manage to spend it all.

In early 2004, while listening to a lesson at church I heard a powerful principle taught which I'd either never heard or never paid attention to before. Perhaps I wasn't ready to receive it until that particular Sunday morning when it hit me with such force that I decided to test it. Before I tell you this principle, let's take a look at Malachi 3:8-11 because it's in here… I just never noticed it before.

"Will a man rob God? Yet ye have robbed me. But ye say, Wherein have we robbed thee? In tithes and offerings. Ye are cursed with a curse: for ye have robbed me, even this whole nation.

"Bring ye all the tithes into the storehouse, that there may be meat in mine house, and prove me now herewith, saith the Lord of hosts, if I will not open you the windows of heaven, and pour you out a blessing, that there shall not be room enough to receive it.

"And I will rebuke the devourer for your sakes, and he shall not destroy the fruits of your ground; neither shall your vine cast her fruit before the time in the field, saith the Lord of hosts" (Malachi 3:8-11).

Most of the time when we read this passage we think of tithing ten percent. But He says we rob God when we do not give tithes AND offerings. Offerings are over and above the 10 percent. While tithing is generally what we give to our church to help it function and provide the building, facilities, utilities, etc to operate, our offerings are over and above the ten percent and would go toward other charitable causes like feeding the hungry, clothing the naked, healing the sick, supporting missionaries, helping the needy obtain education, and promoting good in the world.

I believe that the windows of heaven are not fully opened until we address both tithes AND offerings. If we really want showered upon us so much that we cannot receive it, then we must be generous in our offerings as well. I realize this can be hard to do when you're still struggling with the tithing principle, but it is one of those tests of faith that Jesus spoke of when he said, "If any man will do his will, he shall know of the doctrine" (John 7:17).

Malachi 3 is one of the few places in scripture where the Lord says "prove me." In other words, *test me, try me, and see if I don't do it.* When I heard this, I decided to put the principle to the test and I've seen amazing results. I've also corroborated these results with a friend who has faithfully paid generous tithes and offerings for years. It has been our experience that whatever we give over and above tithing comes back to us quickly by at least tenfold. We looked at what we normally made and compared our increase to the amount we gave in offerings and it was at least ten times the offerings. For example, if you give a dollar, you get back ten. If you give ten, you get back one-hundred.

It's almost as if the Lord is saying, if you'll give Me ten percent of your increase, I'll see that you're taken care of. If you'll give Me more, I'll repay you exponentially. I searched for a scripture to back up this ten factor and what I found was Matthew 19:29, "And every one that hath forsaken houses, or brethren, or sisters, or father, or mother, or wife, or children, or lands, for my name's sake, shall receive an hundredfold, and shall inherit everlasting life."

So the Lord is actually saying 100 times what we sacrifice to Him is returned to us. Perhaps it comes over time or even after this life. Whether it's 10 or 100, you'll just have to do as Malachi says and prove the Lord for yourself and see what your own personal multiplier is. But it's definitely worth trying to see how it works for you. Without doubt, it will come back to you abundantly. As Melvin J. Ballard once said, "a person cannot give a crust to the Lord without receiving a loaf in return." (As quoted by Marion G. Romney, "The Blessings of the Fast," *Ensign*, July 1982, 2)

In January of 2005 when my husband lost his job and decided to start his new business, my initial reaction was to lower our offerings. After all, we wouldn't have his income, and we might actually be the ones needing assistance. It was a fleeting temptation, and then I decided to do the opposite. I'd seen the principles work before, so I decided to put them to the test again. Instead of reducing our offerings, we increased them, and the results were simply miraculous!

Our monthly expenditures reduced, and our revenues increased exponentially. Financially speaking, without my husband employed outside the home, we were better off than we were with him working at a job. It makes no logical sense, other than the simple fact that the Lord meant it when He said to test Him, try Him and prove Him. He really will open those windows of heaven! I have seen them open, and I stand in awe at His majesty and power!

Fourth, Express Deep and Heartfelt Gratitude

There is no attitude that will draw you closer to the Lord than gratitude. I've already discussed gratitude in depth in chapter six, but I cannot overemphasize its importance. Gratitude is an antidote and prevention for the sin of pride. As you put into action these principles, never neglect to acknowledge that the blessings you receive as a result come from God. They do not come from you. You are not the source of your blessings. It's not your ingenuity, your determination, your skill or perfection that makes any of these blessings possible. It is the Lord, His laws, His blessings and His power that makes it all available to you.

Once we receive a little success, abundance and prosperity, it is human nature to pat ourselves on the back for a job well done. Eventually, there's even a tendency to assume we did it all on our own. In this state of ingratitude, we in essence cut the wires that connect us to God. As a result, we are left adrift on our own. And surely as the Proverb states, "Pride goeth before destruction and an haughty spirit before a fall" (Proverbs 16:18).

Points to Ponder

· Name some times when you were blessed for giving generously. What blessings have you received from tithing or donating offerings?
· How have you been blessed when you obeyed God's laws and commandments?
· How can you stretch your generosity to the Lord and others? How will you strive to live the laws of tithes and offerings and sowing and reaping?
· How will you relax your grip on the things of the world and trust in God's abundant ability to provide everything you need when you need it?

Conclusion

The only reason we want things or events to happen in our lives is because we want the feelings associated with them. We want love, happiness, harmony, security, romance, excitement, pleasure, or some other emotion we've identified with the objects, people, relationships or ideas we seek. Some emotions are more worthwhile than others. We should prayerfully identify and evaluate our root desires to determine which ones are worth pursuing and which are not.

Once we've done that, and are clear on which worthwhile emotions motivate us, we should seek to feel those feelings as much as we can in our present environment – even if we can only feel them on paper or in our minds. As we do this, we will draw the people, events and things to us that promote those feelings.

Focus + Faith + Feeling = Results

Anything in life is drawn to you when you apply your focus, faith and feeling to it. Whether it's wanted or unwanted, if you're giving your focus, faith and feeling to it, you're drawing it into your life.

This is why it's so important to release the negative emotions of worry, fear and doubt. They feed what you don't want and actually draw it toward you. Surely no one wants to feel worried, fearful or in pain. So why do we focus on and create those emotions in our minds? By doing so, we only draw events, people or things to us that make us feel anxious, frightened or in pain!

Focus your emotions using faith, gratitude and a clear vision of what you want and your purpose for achieving it. Then, you will be feeding the feelings you want and drawing them into your life. Remember, your focus is deciding "what" you want. Get specific. Get clear with details about what you want. Feel as if you're already in possession of it; be grateful for it ahead of time!

Your feeling is deciding "why" you want it – what feelings will you experience when you have what you want? Feel those feelings now! Don't wait to experience them at some later date. Identify the emotions you desire in your life and pull them out of your existing environment, relationships and experiences. They are there. If you're not seeing them, perhaps you aren't "being still." Or if your circumstances are just so contrary to the feelings you want to experience, close your eyes and imagine what your life will be like and look like when you feel how you want to feel. Seek out and feed anything in your present environment that fosters these positive emotions.

Your faith is letting go of the remaining questions for God to handle. Faith is knowing that all things will work together for your good in the appointed time and way. You express your faith through deep and sincere gratitude for things as they are right now and as you know they will be.

The quicker we let go of the things that are out of our control, the sooner we'll relax and be free to fly. Listen to the Spirit. It is your guide and will prompt you in how to act and what to do. Trust the good desires of your heart. Anything that is virtuous, lovely, of good report or praiseworthy, anything that lifts, builds or makes the world a better place is a righteous desire. Those desires are planted in your heart by God. Don't bury them! Feed them! Get clear on what you want, why you want it, and give the details of the how, when and where to your Heavenly Father.

As you consistently act immediately upon each and every prompting given to you by the Spirit - regardless of how afraid you may be to do it – your desires begin to take shape into physical realities. As you come to trust the Lord fully, you will find that "peace that passes all understanding," and what you want will distill upon you as the dew from heaven. Worry will become a thing of the past because now you know how to ask intelligently and specifically. You have a clear distinction between what you control and what God controls. Most importantly, you know you are a child of God with a wonderful future and a divine plan that He desires to assist you in fulfilling.

So trust! Release worry, and
with gratitude and faith,
spread your wings and fly!

Formulate Your Big Picture: Your What & Why

What do you want from life? Why do you want it? Paint a picture of how your ideal life will look, feel and be. Write it in the present tense and date it at the top like a future journal entry. Then pray and get God's confirmation that you're on the right path. Tweak as necessary with the Lord's help.

Date:_____

I am so happy and grateful now that

_____

_____

_____

_____

_____

_____

_____

_____

_____

_____

_____

_____

_____

_____

_____

_____

_____

_____

_____

_____

_____

_____

_____

_____

_____

_____

_____

_____

_____

_____

_____

_____

_____

_____

_____

_____

_____

_____

_____

_____

_____

_____

_____

I am excited, thrilled, and amazed to see these things
happening in ways that are for the highest good for me and
all concerned. Thank you!

About the Author

Marnie L. Pehrson was born and raised in the Chattanooga, Tennessee area and lives with her husband Greg and their six children in Northwest Georgia.

Marnie is the author of inspirational nonfiction works such as *Lord, Are You Sure?*, and *10 Steps to Fulfilling Your Divine Destiny* as well as historical fiction titles including *Waltzing with the Light, Hannah's Heart, Beyond the Waterfall* and *The Patriot Wore Petticoats.* She also writes new ebooks regularly for www.CleanRomanceClub.com.

Marnie has served in many capacities in her Church with the young women's, women's and children's organizations. She has also served as a Family History Consultant, Gospel Doctrine teacher and is currently a youth Seminary instructor.

Marnie is the founder of multi-denominational SheLovesGod.com. The site hosts the annual SheLovesGod Virtual Women's Conference the 3rd week of October each year. She's also an accomplished Web developer and entrepreneur. You may reach her through www.MarniePehrson.com and www.PWGroup.com or by email at marnie@pwgroup.com or by phone 706-866-2295.

Books by Marnie Pehrson

The Patriot Wore Petticoats

Historical fiction, 224, pages, ISBN: 0-9729750-4-7
Daring "Dicey" Langston, the bold and reckless rider and
expert shot, saves her family and an entire village during the
American Revolution. Having faced British soldiers, rushing
swollen rivers, the "Bloody Scouts," and the barrel of a
loaded pistol, nothing had quite prepared this valiant
heroine for the heart-pounding exhilaration she'd find in the
arms of one brave Patriot. Based on a true story about the
author's fourth great-grandmother. Learn more at
www.DiceyLangston.com

Hannah's Heart

Historical Fiction, 108 pages, paperback, ISBN: 0-9729750-6-3
Hannah Jamison made the mistake of falling for the wrong
man. Not only did he find her irritating and troublesome, but
also her father had no use for him. All seemed a hopeless
infatuation until Mother Nature threw the two together in the
perfect time and place. But now what to do about her father?
Based on a true story about the author's great-grandparents.

Beyond the Waterfall

Historical Fiction, 136 pages, paperback ISBN: 0-9729750-7-1
Jillian's feet were precariously planted in two worlds: the
Cherokee nation on the brink of extermination, and the world
where he belonged. On her first meeting with the charming
and handsome merchant, Jesse Whitmore had set her young
heart ablaze. Yet, could she trust him? Or was he just like all
the other white men she'd encountered? Would he stand
beside her while she witnessed her nation ripped apart, or
would he join the ranks of the powerful greedy to betray her?
Based on family history and local legend.

**Visit www.CleanRomanceClub.com
for more of Marnie's titles in ebook format**

Waltzing with the Light
Historical fiction, 268 pages, paperback, 0-9729750-5-5
Nestled within the valley of the Appalachian mountains,
Daisy, Tennessee, seemed like a sleepy little town until
depression-era drifter, Jake Elliot, entered it and knocked on
the front door of the yellow farm house and met Mikalah, the
oldest of the Ford children. Little did he know how his life
and his heart would be affected from that moment forward.
Although Daisy seems peaceful and inviting, for a member of
the LDS faith it has its ruthless characters and dangerous
moments which threaten Jake & Mikalah's plans and their
very lives. The misconceptions over Jake's beliefs test the
metal of everyone he encounters, bringing out the best in the
most loveable characters and the worst in those with more
treacherous motives.

Lord, Are You Sure?
Inspirational, 152 pages, ISBN 0-9729750-0-4
A roadmap for understanding how Heavenly Father works in
your life, helping you understand why certain problems keep
repeating themselves, how to break the cycle and unlock the
mystery of why you encounter challenges and roadblocks on
roads you felt inspired to travel.

10 Steps to Fulfilling Your Divine Destiny
Inspirational, 124 pages, ISBN 0-9676162-1-2
Have you ever said to yourself, "I'd love to do great things with
my life, but I'm just too busy, too untalented, too ordinary, too
afraid, too anything but extraordinary"? Inside this book you'll
learn the 10 steps for discovering your life's mission.

A Closer Walk with Him
SheLovesGod Study Lessons Volume 1
Inspirational, 212 pages, paperback, ISBN 0-9729750-3-9
A collection of insights and ponderings on the scriptures and
how we can apply them to our everyday lives. 52 Lessons.

**To order call 800-524-2307 or visit
www.MarniePehrson.com**

www.ingramcontent.com/pod-product-compliance
Lightning Source LLC
Chambersburg PA
CBHW031320040426
42443CB00005B/150